FRANKLY
SPEAKING

FRANKLY SPEAKING

A BARTENDER'S VIEW OF THE WORLD

by
Frank Levans

in collaboration with
Dr. Ramakrishna Puligandla

Frankly Speaking: A Bartender's View of the World

Published by Hats Off Books®
610 East Delano Street, Suite 104
Tucson, Arizona 85705 U.S.A.
www.hatsoffbooks.com

International Standard Book Number: 1-58736-479-4
Library of Congress Control Number: 2005924499

CONTENTS

FOREWORD

We have all, at some time or other, heard someone say, "What planet is he coming from?" when someone makes an observation or states an opinion that is quite different from those held by most of us. But suppose "someone from another planet" is actually a person so detached and removed from the maelstrom of conditioning factors that affect the rest of us that it is as if he were from a different planet. The issue is not unlike that of a judge who does not have to recuse himself if/when a member of his family comes before the bench.

More specifically, suppose someone from a "red state" on the political map encounters someone who clearly does not share his/her political views. The person whose views are challenged would immediately assume that the challenger has views consistent with those held by the majority of voters in the "blue states." *What other alternatives are there?*

Similarly, if the referee in a sporting event is a graduate of one of the institutions represented on the playing field, how can he *not want* his alma mater to win?

Growing up is not simply getting taller and heavier. We also grow up psychologically, or at least we ought to. We extend our egos. We aggrandize our egos. And maybe, just maybe, something called "ego maturation" might occur. When ego aggrandizement occurs, as in "John is now aggrandizing his ego," is the verb transitive? That is, what I is the goal? Will his ego ever be completely aggrandized? Is there an end to the process? How would we know? Can the judge attain this level when meting out justice? Can the referee transcend his desire for one team to win and the other to lose? Can Frank, a native of this planet, achieve this level?

Is religion analogous to a leash with us (homo sapiens) at one end and God at the other? Are conservatives on a short leash? Are liberals on a long leash? Are Christians on one leash and Muslims on another? Are different Gods at the other end of the leashes? What would happen if the leashes broke? If God, or the gods, let go?

Plato wrote the *Republic*. Sir Thomas More wrote *Utopia*. And people often preface what they are about to say with the phrase, "In a perfect world." So, at least for the sake of argument, let us assume that "a perfect world" is more than an empty semantic utterance. With this in mind, as you read what Frank has to tell us, ask, would Frank be expelled from the perfect world, or would he be the only one qualified for citizenship?

Robert L. Wilhoyte, PhD

PREFACE

Life is an ongoing and exciting adventure, and there are always things one does not know but needs to know. People from various walks of life write about their experiences, whether as professors, lawyers, doctors, corporate executives, and so on. But seldom, if ever, do we have books by *ordinary* people, people whose occupations do not command authority or distinction but are in a very real sense essential—for example, farmers, barbers, bartenders, plumbers, waiters, store managers, house cleaners, and such. This book is by one who worked as a bartender for more than three decades. Bartending, notwithstanding appearances to the contrary, is a very interesting and special kind of occupation. A bartender, simply by virtue of the position, gets to know a lot of people from different strata and segments of the society. Bartenders come to know things about people that even their closest relatives and friends do not; bartenders are psychiatrists without therapeutic sessions. From their vantage point, bartenders command a view and vision of people and the world not accessible to others. This book is a faithful narrative of the experiences of Mr. Frank Levans, who tended bars of various kinds—the white-collar, the blue-collar, the mixed, and very private—for a long time. I am a professor, an academician, who first suggested to Frank the idea of writing this book; and when Frank decided to write the book, he requested me to be his collaborator, and I most gladly and immediately agreed. Hence this book in your hands.

Frank and I have chosen to present this book in the form of a series of essays and narratives on a wide variety of topics. The topics cover a large range of great human interests: Why do people go to bars? What kind of people are regulars in a bar? What are the differences between a blue-collar bar and a white-collar bar? What is the nature of the relationships in a bar between whites and blacks (minorities in general)? When and how do fights occur in a bar? Do men and women go to bars looking for conversation and sex? What does alcohol do to people? When does a bartender refuse to serve liquor to a customer? Are bar owners held responsible for accidents after customers leave the bar? What about minors visiting bars and ordering drinks? How and why do customers trust a bartender and confide in him about their private lives? These are but a few of the most significant topics, along with sports, politics, the media, and various aspects of life, such as family, schools, and education, discussed in this book.

One might think that one knows the answers to all the questions raised here; such, however, is not the case, for one does not have the rich and varied experiences of the bartender, on the basis of which alone these questions can be answered in a true and reliable manner. The main purpose and chief objective of this book is to provide such answers, thereby enabling the reader to know things of which he or she had only vague conjectures.

If we are even modestly successful in realizing this goal, by providing the reader with a true, faithful, authentic, absorbing, and, above all, most enjoyable picture of a bartender's view of the world, we will have been more than rewarded. Now please read on!

Dr. Ramakrishna Puligandla
Collaborator

ACKNOWLEDGMENTS

We hereby wish to acknowledge our deep-felt gratitude and thankfulness first to Lisa (Levans) Burkhart and our best friends, Marian Crooks, Jodi Lee Kerekes, and Sharon Roselle, in the preparation of this manuscript. We are especially thankful to them for their patience and kindness in revising the manuscript more than once and putting up with our literary idiosyncrasies. We are particularly grateful to our dear friend Kipous Diacou for his full cooperation in the production of this manuscript. We are most grateful to our dear friend Dennis Lindsley for having so generously offered his expertise in the preparation of the final draft and taking the cover photo. We are also most grateful to Professor Robert Wilhoyte for deeming this work worthy of his foreword.

Finally, we are deeply thankful to James Reel and Susan Wenger for their superb editorial supervision in the production of this book. Any faults that may yet remain are entirely our own.

INTRODUCTION

After tending bar and being a frequent customer of bars all my life, I've had the opportunity to talk with and study mainstream and working-class America. Observing people in the bar business and my life's other experiences has helped me keep my finger on the pulse of low-middle America ($15,000-a-year income to the $200,000 two-income family). I want to present a view that most haven't seen yet.

I was exposed to bars at an early age, in the late 1940s, early fifties. My mother was a strong, independent woman who went through a handful or more of husbands. Most were drinkers and Ma enjoyed going to the bar also; she was usually involved in playing shuffleboard, pool, and card leagues that most bars had going back then. And I went with her most of the time.

Years before I was of legal drinking age, I was in bars in Texas, Florida, South Dakota, and quite a few here in Toledo. From the redneck south to the racist west and good old blue-collar Toledo, one thing stayed the same. The bartender usually had an aura, sorta like "celebrity status." The bartender knew everybody's history, good or bad, the latest gossip or rumors, and was expected to have answers to a multiple range of questions, and had the last word in a dispute. Even as a kid, bartenders caught my attention; to me they were "cool."

It was by accident I became a bartender; it was in the mid '60s. Corky, a friend of mine whom I worked with in a factory, was a weekend bartender in a club that had its regulars and a weekend singles crowd. It was a cross between *Cheers* and *Animal House*, with a go-go cage thrown in.

One evening while bending my elbow, bellied up to the bar, Corky, who was busy trying to keep up with the action, since the other bartender was late, asked me to give him a hand (he was desperate). At the time, being a bartender was nowhere in my mindset. I went behind the bar, started opening bottles, emptying ashtrays, washing glasses, and before I knew it, I got right in the flow of things. When the owner came in later on, he told me to stay behind the bar for the rest of the evening. He hired me that night.

I knew how to operate a cash register and handle money from past experiences in my mother's business, and working in a drug store in my teens was a big help. It didn't hurt that I had been a bar dweller most of my life up to that point; I knew the basic drinks. I was so comfortable that bartending came very easy to me. I fell in love with bartending right from the start. I went from customer to bartender in one night.

Throughout the years of serving and rubbing elbows with no-collar, blue-collar, and white-collar people, I've had the opportunity to observe and study people with their guards down. I'd be there when they needed a drink or a conversation; after a while, they'd forget I was there, and I'd become "invisible." That's when my experiences with people became a study—a fascination and hobby with me.

It became commonplace for people to open up and tell me things they wouldn't tell a best friend, family member, or anyone else who was closer to them than I was.

For some reason, perhaps having a trust in the bartender, they would unload their deepest, darkest secrets to me. As the years went by, I enjoyed just being a good listener, that my opinion meant something to somebody. It wasn't too long before I realized that I had become a priest without a confessional booth and a shrink without a couch.

To this day, advice or opinion just rolls off my tongue. Once in awhile, I put my foot in my mouth, but not too often.

I learned more about people from my invisible place behind the bar, more than I could ever have imagined. One of the first things I picked up on still holds true today: Alcohol is not the problem; it's when it mixes with an unstable mind. Like most drugs, all it does is release what is in the subconscious, not create it.

Some Views:

1. I know alcohol doesn't cure stress or depression, but I've seen a lot of people who thought it did.
2. People beat themselves up over the past, not realizing how it ruins their future.
3. The majority of people think the worst in most situations, screwing themselves into the ground, over something they can't control.
4. You learn very quickly not to pry (nine out of ten times it won't take long for people to tell you anyway). Just stand back and smile and pour their drug, alcohol, and you'll be their bud.
5. People have more patience and understanding with strangers than with friends. With friends they argue and cop an attitude, but with strangers they are a lot more agreeable.
6. Don't allow people to put you in a bad mood or alter your mindset. The only one who can do that is you.
7. Don't look for quick solutions and worry about major events that are usually out of your control. Instead, spend time taking care of hands-on, everyday problems.
8. Most people won't admit that they worry about what others think about them, having self-doubt and feeling inadequate because of peer pressure about their clothes, job, hair, whether their car is washed and waxed, etc. They don't realize that they are trying to appease others when making personal decisions that reflect on their overall well-being.
9. People will give a different opinion on a subject when one-to-one, rather than in a group.

10. A person who doesn't believe in giving someone a second chance most likely will never admit his or her mistakes.
11. The majority of people, when told they can't, their brain won't.
12. To some, good can get better. To others, bad will always get worse.
13. Naïve and gullible people take a lot of flack. The ones I have been around are very nice people who aren't worried about having to be on top.
14. Nothing can make a man more nervous than trying to impress a good-looking woman.
15. A large number of people get their knowledge from TV, movies, newspapers, magazines like *People*, *Time*, *Reader's Digest*, or something on that order, without comprehending that they're being programmed with sensationalism and double standards by word-arrangers. TV and newspaper versions of right or wrong are all used for controlling people's mindset and to lead them down the road to markets-ville.
16. I've seen how important it is for people to have the right someone, at the right time, say the right words, using nothing but simple logic, to straighten out a little kink in their life.
17. I realized after every year that passed, listening to people cry in their beer, that I wasn't as bad off as I'd thought I was. Considering the hurdles I got over in my life, through many situations, my mistakes were few and rarely repeated. They weren't premeditated or meant to hurt. Just the wrong decision at the wrong time. My mistakes were all behind me, just like my bald spot. I adopted Popeye's philosophy: "I am what I am."

You learn a lot about psychology in service-oriented jobs. Because of how alcohol affects people, along with being made "invisible," a bartender gets a different insight into human behavior. The psychology I learned tending bar isn't of the university variety (the kind taught for applying control and gaining superiority over others—that most students get along with a degree). It just came to me from the school of life, where common sense gets you a degree, not the use of thirteen-letter words.

"Thought should be the aid to observation, not its substitute," said a great philosopher. I read this ten years after I started tending bar, when my mother passed away from diabetes. That's when I got a wake-up call on taking better care of myself. I started reading a lot about health, which led to psychology and philosophy. Nowhere was this piece of philosophy more helpful to me than in becoming part of my mindset, as it is to this day. It helped in dealing with customers who thought that only what they saw or heard, but not knew, was the real deal. Frankly, it took many years of life's experiences and mistakes for me to realize that my brain is smarter than I am.

I would like to see psychology taught in our public school system, starting in the first grade. Good teachers teaching basic psychology would be invaluable to children, soon to be young adults. Knowing yourself, being comfortable with you as you are, understanding the capabilities and pitfalls the brain has control over going into adolescence, would produce a confident, secure, less violent youth and a stable, less stressful adulthood. The older you get, you'll know this is the only way to obtain real happiness.

In private schools, where it costs to give your children a good education, psychology is part of the curriculum. I guess our public school systems, despite all the tax and lottery money, can't afford the expense to teach philosophy to low-mid American children.

I want to offer a clear and simple explanation that is crucial to understanding preprogrammed thinking, in good old, everyday, low-mid American language, not the double-standard misleading words spun out by the word-arrangers (where right ends up wrong, wrong ends up right, something turns into nothing, and you don't even know what "is" is).

This book could help people become aware of and break the subconscious preprogrammed thinking that hinders a person's thought process. After studying preprogrammed thinking most of my life, I concluded that life would be easier and happier if people weren't being manipulated into making decisions and judgments on and for someone else's reasons.

Besides bartending, growing up in a melting pot of nationalities in North Toledo, my gypsy lifestyle, and dealing with people from all walks of life have helped me keep an open mind, which has enabled me to become immune to most preprogrammed thinking. I still work hard at not falling prey to it (it's like taking vitamins; it takes time to see the results).

Preprogrammed thinking is a form of brain damage. I've been around people who were labeled "retarded," "slow," and so on. People with brain damage don't have the preprogrammed syndrome; they look at life with a simple "nobody's perfect" philosophy.

I have a friend (more than a friend) named Brian who was born with brain damage. His parents, Linda and Larry, are two of my best friends. I've known Brian since his birth, twenty-five years ago. Watching him grow up has shown me how easy it is to be nice. He doesn't hate or lie. He gets upset, but not angry. He sees everybody as a human being, not caring about the color of your skin, your religion, who you voted for, or your social status. Brian doesn't have the preprogrammed, prejudiced outlook that we so-called normal people have. You won't feel sorry for Brian; you'll just like him (even though he is a Yankees fan). Sometimes it makes me think, perhaps we should all have a little brain damage.

Standing behind the bar almost forty years ago, I would hear people's worrisome conversation about America and the world's problems, blaming the wrong people or things for reasons the newspaper and TV led them to believe was the truth. Wanting to know the real story behind the headlines began with me, after reading books about the blatant lies in the Kennedy cover-up (twenty years before the History Channel exposed it).

Time and again, American mainstream information outlets have made conspiracy theories about international bankers, the "new world order," and numerous other organizations, conditioning people to look for fantasies, rather than the truth. They've been misleading and confusing most Americans with a flood of insinuation, deceptions, and disinformation, that the word-arrangers conjure up so most Americans won't take any of it seriously. I take it very seriously. There's nothing new about the banking families (which I refer to as "the Puppeteers") who control the purse strings not only of Americans, but of the world. They have the puppets who dangle at the end of their purse strings worldwide to do their dirty work. I'll just stick to America. These are the people driven by greed and power (the up-front person we see is used or blamed, but hardly ever punished).

The legal profession is the Puppeteers' and their puppets' word-arrangers (W.A.); they have America by the balls, and keep on squeezing, starting in our government from President to Pentagon, corporations, financial institutions, media industries, and every other organization as you go down the ladder of control. The marketing industry sells sensationalism— violence and sex—that they call "advertainment." All this and more would not be so out of control now, without their legal departments' word-arrangers. The word-arrangers are very effective at creating a smokescreen to keep the Puppeteers out of sight and out of mind.

The legal profession's most important tool is the court system, robbing Americans of their rights and possibly resulting in the loss of our freedom. Using their trumped-up vocabulary of deception, they're rewriting our Constitution with regulation, deregulation, revision of amendments, law changes that have allowed the legal profession to thrive and keep on squeezing. Our Constitution needs to be revised fairly, not where it's rigged by special-interest groups that cause low-mid Americans to be pawns of the wealthy. I've been on the banks of mainstream America, but never got more than my feet wet, and knew better than to get in over my head.

Bartending was a rewarding, eye-opening experience. Watching customers languish in their misery over their life failures made my life's misgivings seem like high school stuff. Watching people who appear to be strong on the outside crumble before your eyes, trying to drink away the past, helped me gain confidence in myself and made my life less complicated.

I never dwelled on the dark side of my past. But after years of seeing people beat themselves up, it made me aware of how important it is to erase past mistakes, for one's own sake. By having human guinea pigs to use for research, I believe, it's possible with perseverance that human weakness can be broken down by replacing negative thinking with positivity.

As long as I can remember, I never expected anything from anybody. This has kept me from getting my hopes up too high, and has made disappointments roll off my back. I'm not a loner, but I'm completely comfortable being by myself, which a lot of people can't understand. Material things have been secondary to me; I enjoy giving and helping, and I love to laugh and create humor.

Tending bar was perfect for my personality. There was no bigger thrill than creating humor and getting people to laugh and have a great time (even though I had a captive audience). I've been called a character, "abby-normal" by some. When told that, I had only one thing to say. Smiling, I'd respond that all my closest friends are characters; if they were normal, we wouldn't have had so much fun being "non-sensical."

Life is an open-faced sandwich; if you don't like what you see, don't eat it. *Frankly Speaking* is just my open-minded view, not a my-way-or-no-way attitude. My perspective for some will be hard to swallow. For others it will go down easy. My purpose is to help, to have my views itch people's brains enough to make them scratch. Getting them to search for more knowledge that might help their life be a little bit smoother somewhere down the road will do.

From the time Rama gave me the confidence and push to write this book, my motivation has been to hand it to my two wonderful children (adults, but still my kids), Greg and Lisa, who have been my strength whenever I got weak, and the love of my life. I've embarrassed Greg and Lisa on a few occasions (maybe more than a few), but I didn't disgrace them.

Chapter 1

ALCOHOL

Frankly it's a toss-up between alcohol and nicotine as to which of these drugs is America's favorite, but you will see them hand in hand in any bar or nightclub. From cave dweller to bar dweller, alcohol has helped humans escape the drudgery of survival.

Alcohol has been a part of American culture, just like every culture in history. It's ingrained in our culture now more than ever, one reason being that we're introduced to alcohol at an early age, by grownups, as an adult beverage that's accepted in most family circles. Also, it's subliminally instilled in our youth by the entertainment industry as "cool." What I believe is the biggest factor is Americans' financial ability to indulge in our wants as well as our needs. Frankly speaking, it would be fair to say that there're more homes with alcohol in them than Bibles.

Observing from behind the bar and other areas of my life, I've seen alcohol break down some of our preprogrammed habits that people are governed by when they're sober. You know what people are not telling you by what they *are* telling you. When buzzed on alcohol, people will let their hair down and don't worry much about what people think of them. They're not conscious about being "politically correct." They loosen up on the color of the skin and other prejudices. Introverts become extroverts and vice versa. Quiet people become mouthy and mouthy people will get silent and withdrawn. Some people that are money-conscious (tight) become big spenders: "A round for the bar! I'm buying!"

People who are shy or reserved when sober, after a couple of drinks under their belt, will approach the opposite sex for conversation and maybe even dance when ordinarily they don't. In most cases, after one too many, people can't lie to themselves.

Alcohol is one of the top drugs when it comes to causing mood swings. It unleashes two of our ugliest and strongest emotions, violence and jealousy. It makes some people depressed and melancholy. It brings out the Walter Mitty and Charlie Brown syndrome in most of us. It induces a fantasy state of mind that some people like to go to now and again. It gives wannabes a false sense of courage. When alcohol mixes with people, it can *alter* their thinking, not manufacture it.

Alcohol has been America's number one "recreational drug" since long before the term was ever brewed up. It's as much of America as apple pie, and it's at every baseball game.

Alcohol is used by some people to take the edge off and others to get drunk. It's a relief from the norm, an escape from reality, consumed from celebrations to wakes. Some can't wait to belly up to the bar after work, to have a few quickies before going home. How many Mr. and Mrs. Americas make themselves a stiff one before dinner, have a couple of beers when working around the house, or in the evening with a little butter corn while watching the tube? It's a hereditary trait in low-mid Americans to hit the old watering hole to unwind.

For bar owners in the neighborhood, sports bars, and nightclubs, Friday night is usually their biggest moneymaker. For most of low-mid Americans, when the eagle shits (Friday-payday), going to their favorite watering hole is a tradition that goes back generations. For the young, single, nightclub crowd, alcohol helps make Friday night the coolest night of the week.

For the once-a-week bowler who gets out with friends, alcohol is part of the sport, right down to the old beer frame. Hardly anyone watches the big game without alcohol. Whether you're in a big sports bar with multiple TVs, in a neighborhood bar with just one, or a house gathering, alcohol is there for the kick-off.

"I'm going out for a drink" has been heard by many wives. Besides a drink, there's another purpose behind this phrase. It's an excuse to get out of the house or to get away from the other half to the camaraderie of hanging with the guys to escape the repetition of a routine lifestyle. To many, it's notoriety, like in *Cheers*, when everybody yells "Norm." It was very obvious to me in my first years of tending bar how customers liked when I called out their name when they walked through the door.

When our economy is in a slump (like now), it will affect the sales of most consumer products that are necessary in our everyday life, but not alcohol. People will go without, to have enough to drink.

The alcohol industry is probably one of the stablest industries in America. Their product is a "legalized drug," openly accepted and readily available across the counter. No prescription necessary.

When the government (taxes) and business world make money off the same product that people "need" like alcohol, oil, it obtains immunity from being discredited by the system. It's presented (marketed) to the public with double-standard views. Alcohol is evil when connected to a tragedy, but it's economically a great benefit and a social decorum at a cocktail party.

Most bar dwellers fall into a "want" or "need" category, I'll touch on that in the following.

Myself, I would fall into the want category. I want to get out and have a few drinks and mingle with friends and reminisce with strangers. I don't need alcohol. I don't drink at home unless I have guests and company. I don't drink during the day. When alone, I couldn't care less if I drink. I've been drunk more times than I care to count, but even when I drank excessively, I didn't consider myself a drunkard. What probably helped and gave me no choice about drinking the next day were the glorious hangovers. I would be in *Guinness World Records* if I had counted how many times I barfed.

Regardless of movie and TV sensationalism and bad publicity that blames alcohol for human weaknesses, after years of being around people who consume a drug that can bring out the worst in some, no matter what side of the bar I was on, I believe the solid majority of people are good. But just like everything else in today's society, only the bad get all the attention.

Alcoholics

When it comes to weakness, alcoholics are at the top of the class, and definitely fall into the need category. Most people at one time or another in life have been exposed to an "alkie." Whether family member, neighbor, friend, or fellow worker, I've been up close and personal with alcoholics most of my life: stepfathers, my best friend, neighbors, and many customers.

From my perspective, alcoholism is no more than mind over matter. I don't go along with our bureaucratic medical profession calling alcoholism a disease. I've been under the impression diseases are treated by doctors with medication or surgery. I wouldn't call alcoholism a disease, because I've seen it cured just by using the brain.

The alkies I knew personally were null and void and making asses of themselves or bothering customers, and eventually I would have to physically throw them out the door. These guys were losers with no self-respect, wife and child beaters, who would blow all their money on booze to the point where they didn't have food on the table or clothes on their kids' backs. I've seen these same alkies turn their whole life around and conquer alcoholism with the help of AA and the mental strength it takes to quit. (There are a lot of people with a real disease who wish it were that easy.)

About the time a lot of Americans got Blue Shield or some kind of medical coverage, all of a sudden alcoholism became a disease and another source to fill the pockets of the medical profession.

Alcohol is the anesthetic for disappointment. Alkies keep themselves mentally broken down, and they cop out on life's obstacles with an attitude of "I can't do it." They use the drug alcohol like any other drug addict, as a crutch to stay mentally crippled.

People's acceptance of alcohol first caught my attention when I was a kid. People would feel sorry for the neighborhood wino. When talking about him, they would say poor Joe the wino this, poor Joe the wino that. Even today people have a "feel sorry" attitude for alkies.

The same people who are somewhat sympathetic to alcoholics look down on pot smokers, and say things like "He or she is a pothead drug addict, no-good low life." Frankly, most people I've known throughout the years who smoke pot are more responsible and mentally a lot better off than any alkie I ever came across.

Then there is the closet alkie, a real troubled person. They have a bottle of booze hidden in the cupboard, basement, garage, so nobody will find out about their weakness. They get inebriated, start stumbling and stammering, but after a mouthful of mints, they lie to themselves: "That'll work; nobody will know now." I knew a few unhappy housewives and half a dozen husbands like that. They would drop into the bar once in a while to unload their troubles to me. For some reason, locked up in that head, they definitely have a hard time kicking their addiction.

Also there is what I call the "top-shelf alkie," the professional, doctor, lawyer, CEO, executive type. I know after years of serving these pros, they pound fast and hard trying to distort reality. Most don't like themselves or what they're doing. When one-to-one, they start crying how their family doesn't like them, people at work hate them, and they wish they had friends. Ask any bartender—they're the worst tippers, except when they're with their mistresses.

Male alcoholics who are slobs piss themselves, are dirty, stink, and are an ugly sight. But the most disgusting thing to me is to see a female in that condition. Maybe, because being a male, I think of her as being someone's mother.

Drunks

Drunks are for sure in the "want" category. They want to be mealy-mouth stupid assholes, and accomplish this with the use of alcohol.

Alcohol is their potion used to put them in a different mindset, to escape from being someone they don't like when they're sober, "their self." Drunks change with every drink, mostly get mean, like Dr. Jekyll and Mr. Hyde. The Dr. Jekyll person comes in at 9:00 p.m. with a cordial "Hi Frank, how are you tonight?" By 11:00 p.m., about the time you're humping with two deep at the bar, Mr. Hyde comes out and gives you a "Hey, can I get a drink in this *fuckin' place?*" You want to grab them by the shirt and slap them a few times. But you don't, for it's part of the business dealing with drunks who work hard at being a pain in the ass.

Ninety percent of drunks have a nasty disposition caused by something in their past or something that's out of their control. Sooner or later, they open up to the bartender and talk about all the reasons they hate life. Most drunks have the same characteristics: deep depression, they go out of their way to hurt and be mean to people, they're moody (which is usually a bad mood), they get belligerent and like to fight, win or lose (makes no difference), they're control freaks using physical and mental abuse on loved ones. All the ways that highlight their insecurity and weak character they try to keep hidden away. That's why, when drunk, they like to make others as unhappy as they are.

Women who are habitual drunks have the same brain-dead characteristics as men. When women turn into a Mrs. Hyde and become mouthy, mean bitches, even if they're attractive, the only guy who can be around them is a Mr. Hyde. Because they lose their self-respect, they're eager to get in bed. But you've got to hurry, before they pass out on you.

I've been using the word "drunk" throughout this chapter; there is, however, a difference in being a drunk and getting drunk. A bartender knows the real drunks; they have "asshole" imprinted on their foreheads.

Frankly speaking, they should have a bar just for drunks, a big neon sign that reads "Jack-offs," with a drunken bartender, and filled with a bunch of drunken, brain-dead, miserable, asshole customers being stupid.

Happy Drunks

They're not in a "want" or a "need" category. I do know one thing: They're a bartender's delight. Biggest share of happy drunks are introverted, but after a few belts, they have more fun than anybody in the bar. They're like the court jester; people around them loosen up and have a good time.

Happy drunks are loud but not mouthy, hardly ever get upset or belligerent. Basically, they're nice people; the alcohol helps them get silly and entertaining. It gives them a little kick-start for that part of the brain that wants an audience to work with.

My first three or four yeas of tending bar, I was lucky enough to work in a bar where the regulars were the zaniest bunch of characters I've ever seen in a bar to this day. Humor was served with every drink. I was broken in tending bar by two of the most hilarious showmen you could find anywhere: Corky (250 pounds), banging on a cooler lid, singing and dancing behind the bar, doing impressions, telling dirty jokes; and Dick (300 pounds), putting cigarettes out on his tongue, pouring liquor on his bald head and catching it on his tongue as it ran off his nose, dancing in a go-go cage in just his boxer shorts. (Picture 300 pounds getting down to "Woolly Bully.") They were masters of the one-liners and playing on people's conversation with suggestive sexual comments, without using XXXX words (my best friend, Corky, can still make me and a room full of people crack up, forty years later). The fun part of the business I picked up from these two jolly giants; it was invaluable to me and my customers throughout the years, wherever I would tend bar.

Believe me, *Cheers* had nothing on the Parkside, which was renowned as a crazy place filled with people who were out for a good time. It was my first realization that alcohol could be the nucleus for producing happiness in bars. I wish every bar were full of happy drunks, because there aren't enough happy people. I guess that won't happen none too soon. If people would kick out their preprogrammed paranoia, prejudices, insecurities, etc, just maybe sometime in the near future my grandchildren and I may be able to have a drink in a bar with a happy environment.

Social Drinkers

I want to touch briefly on the social drinker. They're similar to the happy drunk and are no problem for the bartender. They're a bit on the quiet side, usually nice and polite, and seem to have their act together compared to the average bar dweller. Social drinkers don't need alcohol to change their mindset. They're looking for conversation, companionship, dancing, and, a great deal of the time, the opposite sex. Where else but a bar could a person find that kind of variety?

Binge Drinkers

Binge drinkers are in the "need" category. Binge drinkers are usually in a decent income bracket and have their life in order. Their need for alcohol is always in them; that's why they are afraid of that first drink. They go on drunken binges so they can lose control and go to la-la land. Alcohol takes over their brains and temporarily hides their pasts that they can't change, their problems and dislikes in the present. When the pressure gets too great, they go on a lost weekend.

Binge drinkers usually don't get mean, because they're busy pouring it down until they become a sloppy mess. I never served customers when they were wasted, but binge drinkers would be all right one second and blasted the next. Once they were wasted, I would make their drinks with just a splash and they wouldn't know the difference. (Binge drinkers drank the hard stuff; beer wasn't quick enough).

Binge drinkers will have two or three cigarettes lighted at once and repeat themselves incoherently. They get drunk fast but have tolerance for alcohol. A lot of times, they end up with a form of amnesia (so they say). They come up with "Did I say that? OH NO! I didn't do that!" When they sober up, they become guilt-ridden and think they are alcoholic. I'd tell them, "Look at it this way: You're a good person, not a loser. You hold down a job. You can afford to leave a tip; alkies can't."

Functional Alcoholics

Functional alcoholics, that's a tricky one, but I would say they're in the "want" category. "Functional alcoholic" is a word-arranger term they brewed up twenty or twenty-five years ago or so. I have known functional alcoholics; they all say the same thing, because the word-arrangers have preprogrammed them to think they're alkies. My view is, it's a bad rap. Functional alcoholics begin drinking in their teens. True, they have a drinking problem. Unlike a weak alcoholic, they work, pay their way through life, and handle responsibility. They will drink all day if they can, right up until bedtime, get up, go to work, and take care of their survival needs. Alcoholics don't have that kind of self-fortitude. The big difference that stands out to me is, functional alcoholics can afford to drink, and alcoholics can't.

There are so many instances in which I gained knowledge about the transformation brought on by alcohol to people's behavior. That started behind the bar and carried over into other areas of my life. After years of observing, my view is, if a survey were taken on the pros and cons of alcohol, its beneficial use would outweigh its use for self-pity and self-destruction.

Chapter II

WOMEN

In the past two or three decades, women have become very knowledgeable and able to exercise their rights, and have made larger advances in womanly freedom than in the previous hundred years. From the blond on the subway vent, almost giving you a peek at her touch-me-not, to the blond running across the stage grabbing her touch-me-not.

Men have always controlled women; if a man doesn't admit that, he's either out to lunch, or he won't let his preprogrammed brain fess up to it. Women who were once dominated and controlled by men started to show that they had lives as independent women, began making a fair wage, and gained all the other perks of the sexual revolution. It scared the hell out of a lot of men. Women were supposed to be prim and proper; "ladies don't do that," etc.—all the preprogrammed man-made rules. You hardly ever heard a woman say "fuck," but today the women I'm around in bars and other areas use it more than men. I've had a better position than most to watch, hear, and get close to a lot of women, and being raised by a knowledgeable mother and having two older sisters is also an advantage in gaining insight into women that a lot of men haven't had. "I love the scent of a woman—HOOH-AAH" (from *Scent of a Woman*).

This is something I didn't realize until years later. In the 1960s, a big percentage of women I worked with in the bars were either divorced or separated with children. Because of watching my mother go through it, I had a soft spot for women in that situation; I knew they needed the money more than I did. Well, I wouldn't take my share of tips, so without finances being involved, they felt more relaxed and open about sharing their feelings with me. It broke down the trust barrier hang-up. I picked up on a lot of things about women, and one thing I know is that men should stop trying to think for women, and think more about them.

As a bartender, I saw when women started feeling more independent and enjoyed their sexual freedom. I saw it make a bunch of insecure men, who couldn't be the boss anymore, lose a lot of women. They found out that the old formula—my way or no way, you're just a woman—doesn't work anymore. There would be nights when a man would be drinking with all his buddies, using all the macho ways of covering up his real feelings. Remarks like "That bitch was no good," "I didn't need her anyway," "She can't make it without me," and "There's more where she came from" are the usual ranting of the macho man. Then came the night when he would be crying in his beer (just "Mr. Macho" and me): "Oh, how I loved that woman. Oh my God, Frank, what am I gonna do without her, what did I do wrong?" They, the machos, just couldn't see that it's a fifty-fifty proposition.

I knew women who were mentally chained to the home, and after five or ten years of it would have enough. They would start getting out and about, having men hitting on them, telling them how nice they looked, how much fun they were, and all their other womanly pluses. The preprogrammed male domi-nator couldn't figure out what went wrong and most of the time would blame it on someone else's outside influence. His mistake was lack of communication; he didn't treat her like a lady; she was just a wife and the mother of his children, every-thing but a woman. Frankly speaking, men could help drop the divorce rate if they changed some of their ingrained, male, one-sided views. The male-controlled preprogramming of women is falling by the wayside:

• A woman asking a man to meet her for a drink: Today it's no big thing. But twenty years ago if a woman asked a man to meet for a drink, he would get a half a woodie in a heartbeat. Every now and then I still run into a man with that preprogrammed mindset.

• Man's a "stud" and Woman is a "slut": Men can be screwing two or three women at the same bar or sometimes at work, with everybody tuned into it. He's called a stud and even some of the women think it's cool. If a woman goes home or just leaves the bar with a man, she's a slut. I have known women personally who would be having a little thing on the side (usually because she wasn't getting enough woodie at home or from the other man in her life). Most customers, after her back was turned, would start using all the slut and whore slams. But not the cool dude; "He's the stud."

• Hookers: My mother had a saying she would tell my sisters' young friends who were about to be married. It was considered a formula for a successful marriage: "A woman should be a lady in the parlor, a mother in the kitchen, and a whore in the bedroom." I have known and been friends with quite a few prostitutes in the last thirty-five years. I had sex with some (with no money involved), for we just liked each other. Besides bartending, I managed a hotel for a short time, which had some "ladies of the night" as residents. I have talked for hours with these women and young girls. Some were mixed up on life or drugs, but a lot more of them than people think are more mentally secure than a lot of women I knew in other areas. Some don't like where they're at, but at least they know where they're at and not lying to themselves. A lot of young girls who could be getting a good education are preprogrammed to this life of prostitution and drugs. Instead of using money for education and ways to make their life better, we waste it on things like catching a man on camera with a prostitute (who turns out to be a cop), so *60 Minutes* can brag to people how they exposed the crime of the century, so media conglomerates make some more money. By the time the poor soul gets out of it, the legal profession will make some money, too. The word arrangers aren't cheap. We spend billions in foreign countries to help them fight the drug war and most of that ends up in someone's pocket. We waste it on the bureaucratic system, with things like investigating committees and legislators to oversee other legislators. I think you get the picture. Frankly speaking, there will be prostitution as long as man gets a woodie. Some men like a whore in the bedroom.

• Battered women: While I tended bar, the battered women I talked to were so degraded and abused that they were afraid to make a change. Their men would threaten them with, "I'm going to kill you if you ever leave, bitch." Or beat them up so bad at times that the fear factor was so great that they were too scared to even think of boogying. I grew up seeing my mother fight with a few of my stepfathers. Her having a sharp tongue and a strong will led to some wild and wooly moments. I know first-hand the traumatic feeling and how it makes you sick all over. In my mother's case, when it got to the point of screaming and hitting, she would unload them. When I was a sophomore living in Dallas, Texas, I came home from school one day and saw my mother had the U-Haul hitched up to the car (whenever I saw the U-Haul, I knew we were relocating). We had it loaded and were on our way back to Toledo in a matter of hours. I always wanted to see the look on Carl's face when he came home to that empty apartment. (I guess that's one of the reasons I had so many stepfathers.) That's why it was hard for me to comprehend why women would stay with men who battered them. But unless you're in the state of mind where fear won't let you build the courage it takes, you can only wonder. It's a strange subject. Frankly speaking, a man who treats a woman like a piece of shit, nine out of ten times, saw his father do the same thing.

• Women's lib: When women's lib started, it had good intentions. But now it's so politically corrupt, it is like any other movement. When it gets to the point where it becomes a voting block or anything the system can get its hooks into, the leaders make decisions based on financial reasons instead of on what is right or wrong. I think a woman who can think for herself and use that good old brain she possesses doesn't need women's lib. Maybe, she just needs another woman to talk to once in awhile. The women's lib organization has developed a mindset in women that is as wrong as the years and years of man's domination were. Trying to make a quick change will not do it. History has proven that quick changes can be harmful, even with good intentions. I'm all for women's equality; man and woman should be like a lot of things in life: down the middle, neither too much one way nor too much the other. I wonder if it would still be women and children first, if the Titanic sank today?

• Job market: Women are still being exploited in the job market. I know women are getting better job opportunities than in the past, but, most of the time, they're not getting equal pay unless they work in a union shop. Take the news industry; there are more women on TV doing news than men. Besides less money being paid, the industry is marketing sex. Beautiful and sexy women who are good readers help the ratings and if you're a woman and happen to be good looking and belong to a minority, that doesn't hurt, either. Frankly speaking, if you turn off the TelePrompTers, I think most of them would be in trouble.

• Emotion: Women are the most emotional critters I have ever been around. As the old saying goes, they carry their emotions on their shirtsleeves. That's good, for it's part of being a woman. Men are taught to keep their emotions inside and are expected not to break down or cry, a preprogrammed requirement. I had a girlfriend I used to call "Mother Nature." I called her that because she could be sunny now, and dark and stormy in an hour. Women are that emotional and unpredictable. I guess that is why it is called "Mother" Nature. Because of my relationships with a lot of women, I have had men ask me for advice on the subject. I would tell them, with a smile, "Yeah, I'm an expert on women, and I don't know shit about them." We're wired different. Me man, you woman. Why ask why?

• Rosie: Back in the 1960s, I had a customer named Rosie. She was in her late sixties and looked like Granny from *The Beverly Hillbillies*, about ninety pounds soaking wet. At the start of the evening, she would be nice and polite and order a drink. She would reach down in her sock or in her bra (if she was wearing one), pull out a little lace handkerchief, and pay you, looking like a sweet little old lady. Well, Rosie drank gin, which is the mind killer of all alcohol. As the night wore on she would turn into the wicked witch of South Toledo. She would throw phrases like "mother fucker" and "fuck you, cock sucker" to other customers or Corky and me behind the bar. I worked with men in the factory who couldn't hang with her mouth. One night I cut her off, took her glass, and told her to leave. While I was walking away from her, she hit me in the middle of the back with an ashtray. She had a good arm for a tiny thing. I came around the bar and had to wrestle her out the door. She was a handful; she kicked me, tried to hit me, and called me every name under the sun. After going back behind the bar, I leaned over to one of the customers not seated close to Rosie, a good-looking man about forty, and said, "How would you like to roll over in the morning and see that?" Before he could answer, Corky grabbed me by the arm, and dragged me to the other end of the bar and said, "Frank, that's her husband." I learned something that night that I read in a philosophy book years later: "Thought should be the aid to observation, not its substitute."

• Women with children who frequent bars during the week: The women out partying and staying out half the night while their children are home alone or with some kind of sitter upset me now as they did thirty-five years ago. The kids I watched grow up with a mother like that got a bad start in life. Most of them loved their mother, but didn't respect her. Their moral values are distorted, they reject authority, lack self-confidence (even though they try not to show it), and have trouble in school. They either get into crime or knock somebody up or get knocked up. I'm not blaming just mothers, for I know the dad is responsible, too. I'll get to Dad in the next chapter. But the mother out partying too much and not at home with her kids surely doesn't help. One of the things wrong with society today is kids aren't afraid to go home and face a parent, let alone parents. When I got into trouble, the authorities didn't bother me. But I sure was scared to death to go home and face Ma. I could just see myself telling her she wasn't allowed in my room. Frankly speaking, I wouldn't care how pretty she was or if she threw it in my face, if she was a mother like I just mentioned, forget it; "Sorry, not tonight; I'm busy."

• My rubber doll and women: I had a rubber doll that I had more fun with, just by watching people's reactions. Her name was Hortence (come to think about it, she never did look relaxed). I would drive her around the factory where I worked, she and I in our orange coveralls in my maintenance cart. People at work would fall apart. It gave them a happy break, took their minds off their situation for a moment. Pulling up to a traffic light next to a car full of people with her sitting next to me was worth its weight in gold; it got a lot of double-takes and a carload of laughter. Hortence brought something out in a woman that was strange. Some nights I would take her to the bar with me, tie her onto a barstool, and go to work. For laughs, I would go up to her and act like she was flirting with another guy and slap her. The next thing I knew, the girls I worked with would ask if they could belt her and then their girlfriends would take a shot. It would snowball through the bar. Women loved beating her, and the fiery look in their eyes and the intensity of the blows got me to believe they were hitting the girl who took their first love or husband, or just some girl they always wanted to smack. Maybe, it was because they always held back. You know, "Ladies don't do that."

If anyone who reads this thinks I have anything going on with Hortence, forget it. She was one of the plastic types and full of hot air. What was cool about Hortence? She wasn't like some women I have known who are a handful of take and mouthful of gimmie.

I don't care one way or another if a woman becomes president. Male puppet, female puppet, nothing will change for low-mid Americans, for they'll still be controlled by the purse strings of the Puppeteers. (Voters will still have to choose the best of the two bads, and that is democracy!)

There will be women in America who will vote for a woman president because of gender instead of her qualifications. I can't say I would blame them, after centuries of men being on top. The way it looks right now, our ex-first lady could be that woman. Please ladies, do some research on this matter. Her money machine is counting on women to vote with gender in mind, instead of knowledge of the candidate.

One thing I'd like to reflect on: To her and Willie-boy, catering to Chinese conglomerates for campaign money, wining and dining them and letting them stay at the White House was bad enough. But allowing them access to high-tech companies, an action that will be detrimental to America in the future, is not in the best interest of American taxpayers.

Women voters, China is a country where their government still does little to stop killing baby girls because they consider them of no value.

I've not only been lucky but cherished having the opportunity for long-lasting friendships with women; the conversations I've shared with them were just as rewarding as those with my male friends. Frankly speaking, fantasizing about women is like sipping from the fountain of youth. The most important woman in my life was my mother; her influence on me is indirectly responsible for my writing this book.

Chapter III

MEN

I couldn't have been in the position to put this book together without the male customer. The bar business could not have grown into a billion-dollar industry without men. I haven't seen too many women buy the house a round. The neighborhood bar is basically a man thing. But nightclubs couldn't flourish without sex being in the air. And that takes ladies for the men to hit on (unless it's a gay bar).

In the nightclubs I tended bar, the men outnumbered the women four to one. Because the female gives him a thrill, the male customer fills the tills. I know some women who are reading this saying, "That's bullshit." But even though times are changing, things are still one-sided. Having the advantage of being invisible when behind the bar, I observed women talking with their guard down, without men listening. With that and growing up with two older sisters who didn't know little brother had good ears, I acquired the knowledge to eliminate a lot of the male preprogrammed thinking.

Some things I can explain.

• Men who bailed out on their children

To me the only credentials they have to be called men is what they hold in their hand when they take a piss. I know too many men who, because of being bitter and full of hate for the ex-wife, wouldn't be a dad, let alone a father. You will always be a dad, but to be a father you have to be there. A lot of men, after their divorce, didn't take care of their financial responsibilities. But worse than that, they didn't keep in contact or try to stay mentally close to their children. Their heads would be so full of hate and vengeance that the kids ended up paying for it. And not until they got older would they realize that those wasted years were a costly and tragic mistake. And just like some of the moms I knew, the kids grew up with love for the dad, but not respecting dad.

Since I myself didn't have a father, I thought I would be the last person to leave my children. Well, I did, and for four or five years I beat myself up mentally and drank hard and heavy (the guilt has never left me). Even though I wasn't a good father, I still wanted my kids to know Dad was there. Because of help from a great ex-wife and mother, our kids came out of divorce better than most I've seen (our kids were first; it's not that hard to do).

When listening to people talk about their divorces and worries about their children, I would tell them with all the sincerity in my heart, "I wish for your children to come out of it as good as mine." Also, I would tell them not to forget they're raising adults. My ex-wife, Elaine, and I are very proud of Lisa and Greg.

• Men are reluctant to make changes

It's a peer pressure influence that has men paranoid about people talking behind their backs and pointing a finger at them with an "I told you so." It's the possibility of failure that stops them from letting their brains take on a challenge that could make them happier and more confident. Too many men will stay unhappy inside, because of their fear that trying a change is a financial risk. Why hold back the best tool you have going for you? The men who are happy without making changes like themselves, and you don't find them in a bar complaining to a bartender.

Women will say, "The man she married has changed; he's not the guy he used to be." The change he made was out of context to who he really was. It's like when an animal struts his temporary look to impress a mate. I know men to whom burning bridges is a "no-no." To me, it's just a weak way of saying, "I'm afraid if this doesn't work out, they won't take me back." Frankly speaking, I made a lot of changes and some didn't work out. But I had the satisfaction of knowing, "I tried though, didn't I?"

Most men are afraid of rejection and are somewhat threatened by women. That's a preprogrammed mindset made by not being able to like who they are. If a woman tells them, "no," they think it's because they don't look like the latest male sex symbol. And when women have them outnumbered and start laughing and cutting them up, men take it personally. They usually get mad and start talking themselves into an "I hate women" frame of mind. The fear of rejection is so strong in some men that when they want to dance with some lady they're attracted to, they freeze up. Even when their feet are ready to go, men won't because of that little word "no."

Not all, but a lot of men have to be on top (and I don't mean sexually). Men won't accept equal partnership when it comes to making decisions. They think if their word isn't the last, they're not men. They try too hard to be perfect, have to be number one and make all the right moves to satisfy their male ego.

• Wrong choice of words

I watch men use this approach they get out of old movies. It's no wonder they go home alone. The same old pick-up phrases. "You look familiar; you come here often?" "Oh, what beautiful eyes you have," and so on. The same old lines most women have heard since puberty. He could be the guy she's looking for, but the old first impression shot him down from the get.

• The look in the eye

Growing up in the streets of north Toledo and playing sports with every type of man, "the look in the eye" was second nature to me, way before I got into the bar business. Reading the look in the eye is invaluable to a bartender. When dealing with men who are full of firewater or drugs, their eyes are your gauge to evaluate the situation. With that and knowing the aggressive body language, I was able to cut off altercations most of the time before they got out of hand. It made no difference if they were drunk or high, mad or lying; guys get that pathetic scared look when they're bluffing and about to get their ass kicked. The eyes will show it. The only look in the eye of a woman I was sure of is when they were pissed at me.

Frankly speaking, what makes a bartender nervous is when men avoid eye contact.

• Men who hate their mothers

The biggest share of mother-haters are unhappy, introverted, and mean, and almost all of them are women beaters. This is the type of man who says "I love you" only at the beginning of a relationship when he is trying to get into a woman's pants. He won't or can't trust a woman. She could be perfect and he'll still look for mistrust in his mind. That kind of pre-programmed thinking has led to a lot of broken marriages. Women-haters are about as romantic as a pet rock; they have the sweet lingo of the dominant controller. "Give me a head job, bitch" and "Let's fuck" are just two of their compassionate foreplay lines. Frankly speaking, their brains are on the endangered species list.

• Sportsmanship

One thing I've noticed in today's young men that shows up in their character is that they didn't grow up playing some neighborhood sport with the guys. I mean the body-banging games where you learn about sportsmanship and character.

These neighborhood sports teach a lesson in life men should know. You can be the best on your block and think you're cool, but in another neighborhood, you're just another player. Like the old saying, "Everybody is good in their own backyard." When I was growing up, there were no empty playgrounds or basketball courts like I see now. Young men would be grabbing, tackling, and bouncing off each other. Even the last guy picked or the kid who took his ball and went home learned about teamwork and fair play. As you moved into manhood, it made you better at adapting to changes and handling responsibility. Frankly speaking, men in responsible positions who are competitive yet understanding get much more respect than someone who just uses authority.

The history of man was written by men to impress women. From behind the bar, watching and listening to men jockeying for the attention of a good-looking woman, fumbling all over themselves (been there), I wonder how the saying "It's a man's world" ever got coined.

The physical strength of man has allowed him to govern, make the rules and exercise authority, creating a male gender dominance. True, men have been in control and history has been written through their eyes. What wasn't recorded is how it was influenced by what was between her thighs.

Frankly speaking, the proper and historically correct definition of "chivalry" is: men willing to do it for her, so he can do it to her.

Historically significant men who were in control would lose control over a woman. Whether it was jealousy, vanity, or some other male-ego thing, men have dueled, fought wars, and lost quite a few teeth over women.

Bartenders know better than most how, historically, even ordinary men's emotions are put to the test by a women. When the bride becomes unbridled from the man who rode her too hard, this man sits and stares in his drink, thinking out loud, "What the fuck did I do to deserve this?" Most of the time, it's what he didn't do that put him in this miserable situation. (I know for a fact nothing can make a man lose his cool and go berserk faster than a woman.)

Man is the most insecure animal in the jungle,
All his efforts to prevail will surely be futile.
If we could find one good man to clone,
One who for greed would not turn on his own.
Instead of being the lord and master of his race,
Show his people life and how sweet it tastes.
Instead of looking for something or someone to blame,
Get the world together so we will all maintain.

Chapter IV

FIGHTING

In the bars and on the streets fighting won't let up, until people put more effort into knowledge. Because people are trying to prove how right they are (which usually shows how stupid they can be), you will end up with a better than average chance of violence.

Our system markets fighting to make billions, through TV, movies, sports, media, etc. For the last twenty years or more, we've seen karate movies were everyone gets severely kicked in one of the body parts; professional wrestlers and boxers bloody each other's face; ultimate fighting, men who don't need alcohol for violence, because they just want to show they're the toughest; and the evening news regularly splashing blood all over the front room. These are just some of the ways that made us subliminally accept violence in our culture. Without thinking about it, people will get radical and fight at the drop of a hat and end up hurting someone over next to nothing.

The old John Wayne mentality of punching each other out and having a drink afterwards is unheard of today. Nowadays, if a person gets beat up, he wants to rape your sister and shoot your dog, or vice versa. Fighting has been in bars as long as alcohol has. Only it's worse now because in our society brutality has escalated tenfold, making it easily accepted. I've read and heard that alcohol is to blame. Well, alcohol is still the same as it has always been, only it costs more now.

When fights would occur in the good old days, spectators would yell, "Kick their ass." Now they yell, "Kill the M.F." and "Waste him." That's the mindset of young people now.

When you consider you're dealing with people who have emotional and physiological problems, throw in alcohol, and it's impossible not to have a fight break out every once in awhile in a bar; alcohol is like lighter fluid and a number of things can serve as a match.

Domestic and Sibling Fisticuffs

Couples and family feuds can be the bartender's test of not how tough you are, but how good you are. Whenever you're the third party in this predicament, you're at a disadvantage. If you aren't capable of using the right logic with some soft authority, you will end up in a fight.

Couples' fights were the one kind you couldn't call. Once it got out of hand, you would usually have your attention on the man. But after having a few wildcats on your back, the women you were trying to protect giving you a fingernail facial and a few punches in the back of your head, you gain the experience needed to feel the bad vibes from a couple long before the name-calling and the smack in the face happen. No matter how ugly it might get, nine out of ten times they will kiss and make up and be back again next week. If you were ever around sibling-fighting while growing up, you know if you interfere you can be the one getting whaled on. When dealing with brothers or other male family members, you hope to ease the situation before the fists fly. If you don't, you know your job as a bartender will get you involved into a no-win situation.

Men Who Like to Fight

In my neighborhood, a lot of guys I grew up with liked fighting. Most of them never grew out of it. When they got older and became bar dwellers, they were always looking for an altercation. If someone stared at them, bumped into them, or provided any other excuse they could brew up in their pea brains, they would start a fight. Not caring so much about winning or losing, they just wanted to fight. A lot of them would lose quite often and liked to show off their bloody lips or swollen eyes. It was their weird claim to fame.

When I saw two of these types getting ready to flex their muscles, I'd tell them it's not going to happen in here, take it outside and beat each other's brains out. Men who like to fight will take it outside. They loved to be noticed strutting through the bar on their way out. If I wasn't getting through to them, I would hold up a dime and tell them, "I'm going to call the cops. Then you'll go to jail and end up paying lawyers and judges all your money." It usually worked.

When I started using that type of simple logic, it was in the 1960s. Now it would cost me quarters. Even for men who don't like to fight, alcohol might open a chamber in their brains where violence lives and they will give it a go once in awhile. From my standpoint, most men don't like to fight unless they have no choice. The biggest share of men who are considered brawlers grew up in a violent atmosphere.

Short-Man Complex

Many of the nights I've worked or hung out in bars, I would watch a man of short stature with every shot of Jack and every beer grow an inch and gain ten pounds. At 8:30 he's five-foot-five and one hundred-fifty pounds; before midnight his Walter Mitty mindset has him six-foot-two and two hundred-twenty pounds. Now his little-man insecurity complex has to be satisfied. Inevitably, he looks for a big man to start some shit with. If it's a big guy that's passive, he really gets pumped and acts like he is an animal that has a wounded prey. Mentally he is not short anymore. Sometimes, when his brain is really blurred, he will pick on the wrong big man and after a couple of seconds (if he's lucky) he's picking himself off the floor, realizing he is still a little man.

If you ever worked for or with a man with authority who has a short-man complex, you probably at one time or another wanted to grab him by the neck and punch him in the mouth. (Oops, there went my preprogrammed mind. I'm sorry; bartenders don't do violence). Frankly speaking, fear and alcohol make good companions.

Man-Woman-Idiot

When there's a man with an attractive woman, you can have a third-party problem. This will occur when the third party (self-proclaimed ladies' man) will start flirting and staring at the lady. Before long, the man she's with will notice this and usually get upset. If the third-party dude is somewhat of a tough guy, he not only flirts with the girl, but also gives the hard-guy stare at the man. He goes on his little ego trip thinking how cool he is. If he can work it into an altercation, he gets his jolly off.

Women with roving eyes play the flirting game with the third party. A lot of times, they know they're being stared at and actually enjoy it. Others do it for their own self-esteem. This will lead to trouble if you don't use some bartender psychology to change the women's mindset.

If you know your customers, you can use the right compliments with some humor thrown in without offending anyone. If the woman was just seeking a little attention, which is the case most of the time, I would go into my slapstick hammy entertainment routines, throwing ice up in the air, catching it in a glass behind my back, do a little juggling of whiskey bottles (like they did years later in that *Cocktail* movie). But the one that worked 99 percent of the time: Whatever song was playing, I would change the lyrics with X-rated words. I would do anything I could to keep violence out of the air. Third-party jealousy, which most everyone has seen, is for a bartender like walking a tightrope.

Women Fighting

Now more then ever, women are fighting in bars. For some reason they think it's cool. When the booze kicks in, they get this misconception, "I'm tough, I'm bad." TV and movies pre-program them with the belief that a 115-pound girl can fly through the air and kick two or three guys' asses. In about every movie made lately, a woman punches some guy's lights out. Also, with women lifting weights and taking self-defense courses, this type of hype and sensationalism is very misleading and dangerous.

When a man really gets mad and grabs a woman or when his voice has that rage in it, a woman feels the strength that a man has and becomes intensely scared and shits herself. Gone is the TV- and movie-sponsored image of herself as invincible.

I would rather break up two men fighting any day, than get in the middle of a girl-fight. You can punch a guy if you have to, but a woman, that's a toughie.

Bouncers

It's a job for someone who likes to beat other human beings up. On his résumé it would read, "I like to wear tight shirts and kick people's ass; I think it's cool, man." When I started working in bars, the bartender. would keep control of most situations with authority. Most of the time you had customers or a person who cleaned the place or stacked coolers, etc, who would watch your back and help you throw the troublemakers out. But most of the time, all you needed was your authority. Authority meant something not too long ago (before parents started reading books on how to raise their children), and respect was taught at home. I am not a big man, but authority and being right gave me an edge in most altercations. Another thing that might have helped is that I had their drug.

I know I couldn't control them now, like I did then, because today authority doesn't mean squat.

Then, sometime in the 1970s, clubs get bigger and fighting became cooler, and it became impossible for a bartender to keep control. You had too many weak characters (back biting men) who would sucker-punch someone and run out the door. Sometimes, when two guys would be fighting, people who weren't even involved would try to kick or hit someone who was down. The violent mindset that is prevalent now is that it's cool to hurt someone even if it's a cheap shot. Most bouncers I've been around are borderline psychos. Late bloomers who build themselves up with weights and steroids. Muscle-headed wannabes. Some are guys who come out of the service with their brainwashed mindset, "I'm a tough bad-ass." When they were young, most never got into a real fight, and maybe were picked on by other boys. Now it's payback time.

They like to beat someone up, but not really fight. There's a difference in fighting and taking advantage of drunks, smaller guys, and big guys who don't fight back. If a youngster takes a swing and hits a bouncer, the bouncer will go off because of his macho attitude and work the youngster over, so he can brag about it later, when he and the other muscle-heads swap stories after closing on how bad they are. But when they underestimate their opponent and he turns out to be a tough-minded street fighter who grew up being tough where size doesn't make a difference, the bouncer realizes he bit off more then he can chew. He will back off or run for help. Now he has to fight with a good chance of losing. Very few will take a shot that didn't hurt them and show some brain control and escort the youngster who had a little too much to drink out the door without a lot of violence.

Bouncers and Women

I've seen women hang all over them, thinking how cool they are. But "he's the man for me" wears off fast. It doesn't take long before the women realize how insecure and controlling they really are. I talked to a lot of these girls and they would tell me how this so-called big man ended up being a "my way or no way" woman-beater and was really scared inside about people seeing the real person.

Frankly speaking, we don't need bouncers, but we do need security in nightclubs, as we need in so many other areas of our life today.

When I was growing up in North Toledo, it was considered a tough neighborhood. But like so many other tough neighborhoods in America, now it is considered a violent neighborhood. Bulging population has a lot to do with our violent nature in today's society. At the same time, too many generations have been growing up with parents who are not in the home to teach them manners, respect for themselves or authority, morals, pride, the character-builders for a well-adjusted adult.

Years back, psychologists were blaming cartoons for contributing to violence in children. I grew up with cartoons and watched them with my children, along with generations of other families. Children were not affected by cartoon characters of old, unlike the graphic violence of today's cartoons and video game characters.

Seven- or eight-year-old children are growing up exposed to brain matter splattered across the screen, bullets ripping through bodies, heads lopped off and kicked in, children being slaughtered. This kind of excessive brutality, glorified with the human realism that technology provides today, subliminally produces a lax attitude about the value of human life after adolescence. We should be grateful that there are not a lot more bloodthirsty youngsters out there, given the way violence is psychologically marketed by the entertainment industry and media.

The camcorder-citizen has made sensationalizing violence "a piece of cake" for the media. Take two identical crimes, the one caught by camcorder-citizen deemed significant, while the other is deemed insignificant because of no film to show on the 11:00 news.

Through manipulation of the public by special-interest groups and the legal profession, censorship went from the hypocritical religious chokehold to where the quest for higher TV ratings has the last word. Whether it's morally right or wrong is a matter of no consequence as long as it draws viewers.

Censorship, expression of approval or disapproval, is in most cases determined by social status. Censorship double-standard rules of what should be said and seen in movies and TV have always been confusing to me. Not until the last couple of years could offensive words, such as "god damn," "bastard," "asshole," "prick," "shit," etc. be said on TV. For more than fifty years, there was no problem with "schmuck" and "tuchas" used on the tube. Why is it morally right to see brown African breasts, but not breasts in a wet T-shirt? No frontal nudity, but piles of dead nude bodies. If censorship weren't tainted with the double standards of corrupt powers, it could put a damper on the sensationalized marketing of the brutal violent materials used on TV.

Teens have always been impressionable, impatient with self-doubt, short-tempered, with an "I know that" attitude.

The chaotic lifestyle of the new millennium has produced pre-programmed teenagers with a vicious violent mindset who will brutally attack someone over penny-ante differences. They find out too late that the price of "I'm cool macho" comes at a great cost.

Frankly speaking, the message of the so-called reality TV survival show doesn't help our youth. Honor, sportsmanship, and mental and physical ability lose to back-biting, knife-in-the-back tactics to win.

The fast-paced, payback, paranoid, got-to-be Number One, tunnel-vision mindset in our overcrowded society, along with the sensationalized mayhem marketed everywhere you turn, have people wound too tight with zero tolerance toward others. It doesn't take much for them to overreact with anger and violence. This intense violent nature in the forefront of the majority of Americans' thinking is conducive to the easy acceptance of empty reasons for going to war.

Chapter V

MUSIC

From the cave-dweller to the bar-dweller, music is a spiritual charge used by humans to escape reality. Music can put you in a state of mind that belongs only to you. The right and left parts of your brain are on the same mission—perhaps a trip down memory lane, or your own visual inner journey.

As a bartender, you can see the effect music has on people, the electrical surge that goes from the brain to the body. Feet tapping, knees bouncing with the beat, fingers and hands doing their thing, swaying or boogying in your seat are all involuntary reflexes of happiness. In the bar and nightclub business, alcohol may be the fuel, but music is the adrenalin.

Some of the Things Music Does

Music gets people together mentally. They can be strangers sitting across the bar from each other, both lip-synching the same tune and exchanging smiles. People who can't sing will bellow out their favorite song with friends and other customers. I remember a night when there was a blackout. Some of the patrons lit their lighters and I ran down the street and got a bunch of candles. I didn't want to lose the crowd. Me and a few other people started singing the song "Come on Baby, Light My Fire." For the next couple of hours, before the power came back, everybody in the place sang every song that had to do with fire or light. Thanks to music, people talked for the longest time about how much fun they had that night. It was such a good time that I was seriously thinking of having a blackout night once a month.

• Music is a good way to break the ice. A man can be sitting next to a woman and remark, "That's a good song"; before you know it, they're in a conversation, exchanging views on music, movies, current events, likes and dislikes, their jobs, family, and whatnot. Sooner or later, what comes up most of the time will be a song that brings out the sad tale about his or her relationship that went bad.

• For most males, the main topics are sports, cars, and women. But quite a few times I've seen guys get into a conversation regarding music and talk for hours. They could have been in the bar before, maybe even sitting next to one another. But now, after making this musical connection, they become drinking buddies forever.

• What would nightlife be without music and dancing? It can be fast and sweaty or slow and grinding. Dancing is a form of foreplay that stimulates the libido. "Would you like to dance?" I wonder how many relationships and marriages got their start with that little sentence. Body language and eye contact on the dance floor can say more than words can ever begin to. The old human touch. Music and sex, that's a book in itself. Me and most lovers have their favorite pieces of music to get it on with—classical, R&B, maybe some soft rock, whatever it takes. Music, woman, man make a groovy three-some.

• There's a song for every mood. A happy mood is the norm, but not that exciting. Ask anyone who has worked in a club that has a dance floor and live music. They can tell you about the girl who showed up once every blue moon. She wouldn't be looking for a companion, just wanted to dance by herself. For the ones I served, the standard drink was pop or water. Usually she would be on the quiet side and hardly give anyone a second glance. She would dance for hours in her own little world. Sometimes a guy would try to dance with her, but after getting no response, he would walk off the floor with a puzzled look. She would become a conversation piece for the other people in the place. From my invisible place behind the bar, I would hear all the preprogrammed comments like, "Man, is she out there," "What a loony," "She's screwed up," "She's got a problem," and so on. I wouldn't call it a happy or unhappy mood, but after observing this over years and years, I came to the conclusion that only she can answer what kind of mood she was in.

• You rarely find someone who's in a bad mood in a club on a busy night; there are too many good vibes in the air. But on an off night, there will be someone sitting and staring into their drink listening to a sad song that fits their gloomy condition, and beating themselves up mentally.

People who are a little blue and a tad melancholy, but not bummed out to the point of being down on themselves, will crawl into a tune from the past and get into deep thought (maybe about someone they miss or how their life could have been better). I could tell they weren't mad, as in an "I want to be left alone" mood. Unless they wanted another drink, I acted like I was invisible.

Other Music Odysseys

• At a bachelorette party, women are already on a high note, before they pile out of the limo and hit the club. Music gives it that zing to make it a special event (the stripper helps, too). At a house party or at a club, you gotta have music. The stripper can't grind without it. It's a necessity at bachelor parties, too, along with the films of the great outdoors.

• Music, along with a little help from alcohol, can transform two ordinary feet into a *Saturday Night Fever* happy-feet dance-athon. It also changes Mr. and Mrs. Average America into Fred and Ginger, smoothing around the dance floor.

• Music is a big part of how the modern-day sports industry grew into a billion-dollar business. They weren't happy with just the person who wanted to watch the game. They created fans in their quest for more viewers and higher ratings and made the sport into an entertainment event. For the opening of the Monday-night biggie, they play a high-energy song for hype, to make sure "you're ready tonight." You can't have the halftime or pre-game show at the college level without music being a part of it. The special on the classic game always has the big musical intro, along with the musical effect of the narrator's voice. The special on the big-name athlete has a tune that fits all his moves. The opening show of the Olympics is full of the musical grandeur that gives people the feeling of how spectacular the Olympics are. Everyone knows how music is used in not only sports but in most of all TV commercials. It's a marketing need to help their product succeed. With music in our psyche, it doesn't take much to be used as an instrument by marketers.

• The lyrics of a song reveal to the historian the moods and times of any given culture. Researchers have known for hundreds of years, before rulers altered the truth and facts to fit their status in history, that the lyricists most faithfully recorded events of the day as they were happening. This is why in my generation and today's generation protest songs reflect the times and have such an impact on young people. Rap music is a sign of the times. Too bad it re-created the bad times and did not encourage the good times.

• When I stepped into a bar or nightclub for the first time, I knew by the way customers dressed what kind of music was played in that establishment.

Movies have always made a fashion statement, but around 1955, when I was fifteen, rock and roll hit the scene. About the same time, TV was entrenched in the homes of low-mid America. It didn't take long before the garment industry realized what a marketing tool they had. That's when the garment and music industry started sleeping together.

My generation of teenagers had our cool-looking pegged pants, Levi's and leather jackets, like the rock-and-rollers we saw on TV and movies, whom we copied thinking it was cool. The difference was most of the teens of my day had to pay for them, not their parents.

They used to say clothes make the man. Now the peer pressure that's preprogrammed into teens by the garment and music industry, via TV, movies, etc., makes the man. If teens are not wearing the right labels and logos, they are not part of the in crowd. A lot of other parents and I got our kids clothes that fit the day's fashion, but showed restraint in how much we spent.

The marketing world of the 1980s and nineties used the entertainment industry to make teens feel out of place and full of self-doubt if they weren't dressed like the latest teen idol. That's when parents started paying big bucks and running up more bills to pay for their children's self-determined look, rather than spending more time at home teaching their kids about the value of being yourself. Instead of teaching the word "no," parents spent more time trying to get rich and live above their means. Time became money, and it became easier to hand their teens a credit card. What teen wouldn't want to be able to say, "Charge it"?

My belief at the present time is that the reason most kids like baggy pants is it's a way to save time changing by not having to take your shoes off. It's a mind blower to me that so much money is being spent on clothes that don't fit well and will end up in a garage sale in a year or two. Guess I was ahead of my time. When I was young; I had to wear hand-me-downs that were always too big for me.

Not only are teens making sure they're sporting the latest logos and labels, but also young adults, in order to reach a specified social status, are hung up on fashion as well. I see it all the time when I'm out in clubs. How the self-acclaimed fashionable, trendy, plastic people laugh and make fun of someone not dressed in the latest style or to their liking, and imply anyone is stupid if they don't know who's who in the latest sitcom or the song that is Number One this week.

For the last four or five years, my buddy Rosie and I have been going to quite a few concerts. Whenever we go see one of the older groups performing, we get a charge out of the young people, and kid each other about soaking up some of their energy. I crack up seeing the young people wearing the same style of clothes and jamming to the same music I got into thirty years ago. I think it's cool. Frankly speaking, "cool" is still the coolest word there is. Rosie has been laying this on me for a long time; it's a quote from one of the famous pop festivals: "You miss something in life if you let music pass you by." That might not be exactly how it goes, but you get the picture.

• In a few psychology books, I read how singing a song that you know the lyrics for coordinates the right and left sides of your brain. Using this simple therapy when you're hung up on depressing thoughts that won't go away will relax you, and ninety-nine out of a hundred times you will be much happier than before. This pops into my head whenever I wander into a bar on karaoke night. The odds are I'm going to find a bunch of happy people. You catch people singing a duet with their car radio every day on the road and everybody likes to sing in the shower, but for some people who want more, it's karaoke time.

People with a good voice want to perform in front of an audience or compete against their peers in a contest, just like athletes do. And people with a competitive spirit, when hearing a song done not to their liking, are compelled to do it better, and their kind of talent is appreciated by the crowd. By far, the real crowd-pleasers are the ones who want to be silly and have fun. They don't care about what they sound like or if they're hitting the right notes. All they want to do is get hold of the mike and belt out their favorite song. Their exuberance is contagious, like a happy virus.

But karaoke wouldn't be karaoke without the people you can throw veggies at or get the hook and pull them off the stage—the people who somehow believe they're good, while everybody in the place tries to keep a straight face.

Living in Florida in the late 1980s and nineties, I had friends who were visiting me while on vacation; these people would never attempt karaoke back in Toledo, but they were brave enough while on vacation to get up and sing and have a ball. I watched other vacationers do the same thing. Something about not worrying about who's in the audience sets them loose. People who are usually quiet and stay in the background most of the time can really fool you. My buddy Kenny, with whom I ran down in Fort Myers Beach, was shy and a little self-conscious around girls. After knowing him for two or three years, one night he pops up and karaokes to a song that was a popular pop tune. With girls and strangers watching, he did a great job. After the shock wore off, I scratched my head with amazement, thinking, "I see another Kenny."

My best friend since childhood, Rick, who was like a brother to me, had the basement of the 1970s, with bar paneling, twinkle lights, and the good old lava lamp. Rick, with no electrical schooling, made his own stereo system with parts from old stereos, radios, televisions, and a few store-bought parts. A reel-to-reel, headphones, microphones, and more than twenty speakers gave us all the ingredients to hear your recorded voice after singing your favorite song without the worry of embarrassment.

I called Rick the Great Oz. He would operate his homemade stereo panel just like the character in the movie. After you put the headphones on and started singing, you would go to la-la land and fantasize you were onstage under the spot light. That's when Rick would tape you singing without you being aware of it. That made for some real laughter (when played back) on hearing my singing ability, which sounded something like a crow calling his mate. By the time karaoke became popular, I had no aspiration for singing. I loved to make people laugh even at my own expense, but I didn't have the balls (thanks to Rick) to attempt karaoke. The only song I could ever sing is never on any of the lists they give you to pick from: "Tequila."

• Certain types of music have always been more enjoyable played at a higher volume. However, when rock and roll blasted onto the music scene in the mid fifties, it started a trend that made "loud" not loud enough. I've enjoyed loud music since my mid-teens. That's when rock and roll instilled "turn me up" in my mindset.

The youth of today are driving around with speakers in their cars that are worth more than some of their cars. My apartment is a half block from a teen hangout; they can be a block away when my windows rattle and things on my shelves vibrate. When I hear the booms and thuds vibrating from the car at maximum volume range to deafness, it makes me believe there will be a lot of "Whats?" in these youngsters' futures.

• From the mid-fifties to present day, music is just another one of the extravagant cravings in our lives. People have pushed to the limit trying to have bigger, better, newer stuff than the next guy. In bars and nightclubs, music can soothe the wild two-legged beast when alcohol has aroused the animal in him. The beating of drums, blare of horns, shrill of bagpipes are effective in war to bring the animal out of man. Everybody has a pied piper tucked away in the corner of the brain; how music affects them and their reaction to it vary with the individual.

There might be some misfits who don't enjoy music. If that is possible, they've got to be miserable so-and-sos. Me personally, I don't know of any.

Chapter VI

RACISM

Class distinction probably started when whoever had the biggest cave had the biggest club. To be frank about it, I think racism was implemented in cultures when the power of authority, religious beliefs, and greed became part of the culture. Through wealth-controlling knowledge, they duped others into accepting that they were the masses and the classes. Somewhere in life you had to hear or read, "When we hate we don't communicate." While we're busy trying to destroy each other, a handful of financial controllers in the world are the ones making the real killing.

The American Dream was a sales pitch used to get European immigrants to America. It was a bit of a fallacy, for it really meant "we need labor." In most cases, European immigrants not only paid a price, but had the opportunity to choose if they wanted to leave their homeland. White immigrants faced discrimination, but they eventually would end up with citizenship and freedom, while black immigrants slaved to get here. The slaves had no choice, for they were dragged from their homelands and stripped of their heritage and controlled by the rules and standards of a white Christian mindset. If the black slaves' and white immigrants' color of skin was reversed, there would be no essential change. It still would be labor to create wealth for the controllers.

• Back in the late sixties, when the civil rights movement was in full swing, I was a bartender at a bar on the edge of an expanding colored neighborhood. Black customers started stopping in on a regular basis. To this all-white establishment, it was like shock therapy every time the first few blacks walked through the door. Sometimes one of my black friends would stop by after work, still in his soiled work clothes, to have a drink and unwind before going home. My friend held down a good job, lived in a nice home, and was a good family man. There would be times when three or four white customers would be sitting at the other end of the bar talking among themselves and making comments like, "What's that nigger doing in here, Frank? Who's that nigger?"—the derogatory remarks of the preprogrammed racist thinking of the sixties. Well, two or three weeks later, one of the white men who was making these comments sat next to the same black friend of mine, but this time, my friend was wearing a suit. This guy would be talking to my friend like they were old pals and even buy him a drink. The only difference was he had a suit on instead of a work shirt. Frankly speaking, a lot of people don't want to be racists. They're just looking for something to bitch about.

• The laws of nature pertain to us humans, too. There is not a species on earth that can coexist in overcrowded conditions. To survive, you have to take more than you give. Our lower-class neighborhoods, slums, ghettos, whatever they're called, have expanded mainly due to our government welfare system, which gets people dependent on vouchers and food stamps and has stripped them of their independence and pride. This makes them easy pickings for the leaders, black or white, to mislead them in what to buy, whom to vote for, and what to think. By being on welfare, you support the bureaucratic money-makers who want to keep you right where you are.

• A good education helps, but it's not the total package. In most cases, what's lacking in the life of the overpopulated inner city youth is the knowledge that comes from respecting and admiring a parent, a family member, or an adult with a strong character, someone to talk to face-to-face who cares about their well-being, an adult they trust and who shows by example the strength in being yourself. If they're not fortunate enough to have someone like this, they look for a proxy role model, such as a sports star, entertainer, or some kind of celebrity figure they have no personal contact with.

Black youths whose sense of value is the cool material goodies that they don't have pick a different kind of role model. They pick the one they have first-hand experience with in the hood. This is usually a person of unsavory character.

• When I was a milkman in 1961, I had an area on my route where welfare recipients lived. While delivering my milk, I would hear women sitting on their porches talking about how having a baby was a check in the mail every month. Generation after generation of young girls that have been raised with the mindset that if they get pregnant they'll have an income keeps happening. Young people with a good head on their shoulders will grow up thinking the most important thing in their future will be the mailman.

• There was a very interesting fact I came across in a book a few years ago about a chaplain in a penitentiary who passed out Mothers Day cards to all the inmates; all the cards were mailed out. He tried the same thing on Fathers Day, but very few were sent. This is a good example of the problem, and the importance to young inner-city boys of having a father in their lives.

• I agree people of color have a tough road to travel. But the only way to make it easier is with education and also knowledge passed down by parents. Then maybe the large inner-city undesirables' area that used to be for the downtrodden and losers would shrink dramatically.

• Racism is like baseball and apple pie in America, except it's been around a lot longer. There was an ethnic slur for every race in my neighborhood, and they were all used. North Toledo was a melting pot of nationalities, blacks, Mexicans, Jews, Arabs, and most of the European ethnicities. I went to school with, worked next to, broke bread, and drank with all of them. That's why I'm colorblind. To me, race has nothing to do with good or bad, right or wrong. But I do believe there is a little Archie Bunker in all of us, no matter what color you are.

Not that I haven't made a racial slur when venting behind the wheel or upset about something on the tube or newspaper. But I never needed or used a racial remark when mad at someone face-to-face. If I got mad, it was because they were a dick or I was wrong. Just because you mumble to yourself an ethnic or racial remark when you're pissed off at the moment doesn't make you a racist. The real racist is the person who won't allow his preprogrammed brain to drop its guard.

• Racist beliefs would ease up for adults just by trying a simple method used by preschool children: eye contact. Kids who never knew each other before start by looking each other in the eye. Little tots of all backgrounds can smile, touch, and play together until they get into the school system and before they start copying their parents.

• The black racist is as preprogrammed as the white racist; they can't let go of the past. I don't care what color you are, to think you're disliked because of color will most likely screw up your future. I don't know the feeling but I know the look in the eye from a colored person who hates the color of my skin. When it's no more than just eye contact, I wish I had a way to tell them, "Quit hurting yourself and stop telling your eyes what to see."

• Generally when you hear racism mentioned it's a black and white issue. Hate sensationalism has been used on the screen for the last thirty years to piss audiences off. One of the best ways to keep the racial fire burning is to show a black man kissing a white woman in a movie or on the tube. It's sure to get a negative response from most of the viewers; comments like, "Oh my God, how can she do that? How can her husband and loved ones respect her?" would be whispered throughout the audience. The only one who wasn't negative was the colored man sitting there thinking, "That's cool."

• If you have but one view on any given subject and when it's all the bad things used for hate sensationalism by the word arrangers, where truth is not as important as capturing the audience and the ratings, most likely your decision will be made with a preprogrammed opinion.

• There are three kinds of black leaders. First, you have the kind who push for revolution, the kind who use the media for marketing violence. Then, you have the kind who are part of the political network; they promise more freebies in order to control your vote. They are the leaders who make a lot of money just by keeping people confused and feeling oppressed. Finally, there is the good kind, the ones who speak the truth and point fingers at the people who are really to blame. They teach knowledge and unity as the solution to break the control barrier and gain equality, not hate and violence. When people of color start paying attention to a leader like this, the word-arrangers will try their best to discredit them or ruin them with a barrage of media hype. Frankly, if that doesn't work, they'll assassinate him. In a preprogrammed society, to discredit someone or something is just as easy as to give credit when not deserved.

• If more blacks and whites would read books where they get a better insight into people, read all the facts, pro and con, before making judgements with a preprogrammed thought processes, then maybe your and my grandchildren, after becoming grandparents themselves, will be able to see their own grandchildren not use the color of skin for judgment of the human being inside.

• Blacks killing blacks has the highest statistic of any race. Why do colored people find it so easy to kill one another? (Fathers and sons, brothers and sisters, other family members.) I don't believe it can be blamed on red meat or even their African heritage, contrary to so many of the theories that I have read. But I think it would all but disappear if all the energy that is wasted on hate were used for knowledge instead. If we spent more time relating, we would spend less time hating.

• Scientists have done experiments with rats showing that when living together in an area with plenty of food and space available for each family, there was peace and harmony with no altercations; not until overpopulation, which caused crowded living conditions, did rats become stressed out and violent.

That's when fighting and killing occurred as a means of survival.

• About the N-word: I have heard black men call each other "nigger" all my life. They call each other that more than anyone else does. In sports, at work, or in the streets, I have heard blacks say "nigger" to one another hundreds of times in conversations. It's just a word when they use it, but if that same word comes out of a white person's mouth, that white person is apt to get beat up, killed, or at the least be labeled a racist. It's not the word by itself that they hate to hear; rather, it's the preprogrammed hatred that the word evokes that hurts them the most. White people do not have a word that hurts them as much as the word "nigger" hurts the blacks. The word simply triggers how American history is embedded in the minds of blacks. No doubt it was ugly and demeaning, but the past is past, and if one wants to stay there one probably will. And, with blacks still calling each other "nigger," this will certainly not help its usage disappear.

• An experience that I cherish to this day was one coaching grade-school football for twelve or fourteen years in my old neighborhood. About three-quarters of the boys that I coached were of color, and about 80 percent of them were also from broken homes; most of them had no fathers, being raised only by their mother or maybe a grandparent.

All through my coaching years, the boys would address me as Mr. Levans or Coach Levans. They were never told that it was a rule, or a must to address me that way. It was just a matter of respect that they voluntarily showed to me. Sometimes after practice, I would sit and talk to some of the boys about life in general. Boys would stop by my house and sit on the porch and talk. I noticed that no matter what the subject was, I held their attention. Once in awhile, a family member would ask me to talk with one of the boys who was having trouble in school. I realized as time went by that all they were looking for was an adult male who represented a father figure in their lives.

In the last twenty years or so, I have run into some of the boys I had coached, who have now grown into manhood. On occasion, they introduced me to their children as Coach Levans, with a sense of respect and importance; such occasions made me feel good in that they felt that I had something to do with their turning out to be better people.

These experiences have shown me that discrimination doesn't hold back a knowledgeable individual. A case in point is Mike Bell, the fire chief of Toledo, whom I have known since he was in the fifth grade and was his football coach. Mike came out of the same kind of neighborhood where a lot of the boys would let their race hold them back. I'm sure Mike has faced more than his share of discrimination throughout the years, but his knowledgeable, loving parents, who cared about Mike's well-being, showed him by example the value of education and self-esteem, along with family pride, and that it takes more than bigotry to stop you from going forward in life. Besides the big smile, I still see the confidence in Mike's eyes that was peering out of his helmet when he was a boy.

Beating the odds of growing up with a bad home life was not done too often in that neighborhood, but boys with parents and a good family base usually came out on top.

• I first saw hard-core racism while traveling to Florida with my mother in the early fifties when I was ten years old. Going through the South back then with no I-75, you had to use road maps to travel and passed through a lot of small towns and whistle stops along the way. You couldn't make it through even one of these places without seeing a sign reading "NO NIGGERS ALLOWED—BLACKS USE BACK DOOR," and things of that nature. What was strange is that all the people in the kitchens of the restaurants preparing food for the white people to eat were people of color. There were blacks slaving away on low-paying jobs, as maids, cleaners, etc. in the back rooms of white homes and businesses.

I'll never forget the mean glares and the cruelty in the voices of the brainwashed, preprogrammed Southern racists when giving orders to blacks. Hell, there was a harshness in their voice when they called us "Yankees," because of the northern plates on our car. Having black buddies back in Toledo, like Willie and Gerald, who ate at my house and I at theirs, and played together without color being a factor, made it hard for me to understand why someone wanted to hate a person because of the color of his skin. I came to the conclusion years later that the preprogrammed mentality of hating blacks was bred into Southern whites for economic reasons, cheap labor.

When I was in southeast Florida in the fifties, it was a totally racist environment. A KKK mindset was common and pervasive and anyone other than white people was discriminated against. In the last couple of years when I have been going to Everglades City, I have met some fun-loving good old boys who have taken me four-wheeling and on some boating excursions in the Everglades and to the 10,000 Island area of the gulf. One of the guys whom I made friends with has lived there all his life; he got married in 2001 and I was invited to his wedding. They had a beautiful wedding on an outside deck surrounded by the beauty of the Everglades. After the ceremony, the whole wedding party roared off in an airboat, laughing away about spraying water all over the guests.

Casually looking through the crowd, I saw blacks, Mexicans, and Indians, all shoulder to shoulder with the white locals. Everyone was relaxed and having fun, with no sign of the old Southern racist thinking.

Later that evening, at the reception, while standing around the keg where I spent most of the night, I got into a conversation with one of the guests, a local man in his forties who was a captain of a fishing boat. I was explaining to him how I noticed the difference now from when I first came through the area in the fifties. I said, "You know, you're still rednecks, but the racism doesn't seem to be that bad anymore." He replied with a smile, "Well, maybe sometimes."

• Mexicans have lived with racism imposed on them by the white Christian Spanish Conquerors long before this land was called America. They had to endure the worst of racist discrimination, servitude, and death.

Hispanics in overcrowded living conditions, similar to those in other poverty-ridden groups, were exposed to hate and anger at a young age, without answers or hope for the future. This made violence a part of their built-in survival mechanism. The short-man complex, of which I was aware in the biggest share of Mexican men years before I was a bartender, still exists in their thoughts even today. The old saying that Indians go crazy on fire water could be said about Mexicans also. I'm not saying that people of other races don't get crazy when all liquored up. But frankly, Mexicans are near the top when it comes to getting violent after consuming too much fire water. Not all, but some of my Mexican friends and customers who were good when sober, after the alcohol took over would get a mean, ugly attitude and start looking for trouble. If I would get into a confrontation with them, no matter how well I knew them, I always made sure I was ready when their hand went for their pocket.

I have associated with people of color all my life. At times, my friends of color would be with me in a primarily white environment where I would see the racial stares. And, I have been the only white in groups of color when I felt the racist stares. One thing that I have noticed when I walk into a bar with a Mexican friend is that the stares aren't as mean or for as long as they were if I was with one of my black friends.

From behind the bar and on the streets, I have heard Mexicans called "spic" or "wetback" quite a few times. I know they didn't like it and got pissed off most of the time. But I don't think it has the overwhelming effect like the word "nigger" has on blacks.

Mexicans having a conversation in their own language while being around someone who doesn't understand can be frustrating to some people and make them paranoid. I've seen my buddies engage in it when creating a little humor when screwing with someone they are not fond of. It's also a sly way for revenge and payback toward a racist-minded person, which will usually bring their insecurity to the surface.

In 1956 I was going to high school in Texas. In gym class, because I was a Yankee, the white boys wouldn't pick me to be on one of their teams. So that left me to play with the Mexicans boys. The Texans thought it would piss me off, but little did they know I was much more comfortable with the

kind of people I grew up with. There were some humorous situations that still put a smile on my face when thinking about
them. One was one time when in the huddle while playing
football in gym class, one of the Mexican boys would call the
plays, giving orders and directions to everyone in Spanish, then
look at me (without hesitation), and say in English, "Frank, you
go down and across." The same thing would occur after school,
too. Thanks to my North Toledo upbringing, I never felt out
of place and it didn't stop me from having fun.

Around thirty years ago, the president of Mexico made a
statement in a speech that Mexico will get back the land they
lost to America, without firing a shot. I read recently that of all
the races of color, the Latinos have grown into the biggest
voting block in America. But no matter what their voting
power is, if Latinos don't make education the number-one
priority for their children and obtain knowledge about our
word-arranger system, they will waste their vote on a politician
who works behind closed doors for the system and who will
keep them feeling ashamed and inferior about the color of
their skin.

• Muslims have been living in America for generations, but
now after September 11, it's their turn to be used by the media
to sell hate by spewing racism. People are blaming the whole
Arab race without thinking, just reacting to a one-sided view
presented by the mainstream media pushing the hate buttons.
If you want to hate Muslims with your only reason being
September 11, then you'd better start hating every race and
nationality in America, because I can't think of one race or
nationality in America that at some time in history hasn't
slaughtered innocent people with religion as the primary
motive.

Religious persecution has been the forerunner of discrimination and racism. Religion is a subject you don't want discussed in a bar; it can get nasty. Personally, it's one subject I
don't care to mess with. As a bartender you know there are too
many versions of God, and each is right to someone.

People who wear "religious blinders" are some of the worst
racists I have ever waited on, whether Catholic, Protestant,

Jewish, Muslim, Hindu, Buddhist, and so on. Religions instinctively preprogram negative feelings toward people whose religion is different from one's own.

Chapter VII

DRUGS

Illegal street drugs, along with alcohol (America's Number One legal drug), are not the whole enchilada; it's a matter of how an individual handles them. Some people like to get a little buzz to take the edge off. Others want to get whacked out and go over the edge. My exposure to drugs as a bartender and as someone who likes the night life and parties has enabled me to have an open-minded perspective on the subject. Many attribute drug use to a weak character or bad morals. Condemning someone for drug use is a never-ending crusade. But who in America hasn't at one time or another used some kind of drug, either alcohol, nicotine, caffeine, prescriptions, or street drugs?

The war on drugs, just like all wars, makes the financial backers tons of money, with the everyday people paying the price for it. Drugs have flourished because tax-free money made it into a big business. Anything the consumer uses a lot or is dependent on can be marketed for big profit, and big business will control it.

You see or hear about the big drug busts: a van at the border with six hundred pounds of pot or three hundred pounds of cocaine, speed-boats and small planes with bales of drugs. What we don't get to know about are the ships and big cargo planes that bring to America drugs by the tons. With that much tax-free money to be made, it's easy to pay people, from customs agents all the way up to top officials, to look the other way. Every few years you might hear of a big shipment getting busted. It's just a ploy to keep the voters happy. What's really going on? The drug cartels that are fighting each other to be number one set up the opposition to get caught. Once in awhile a load is sacrificed to make it look like our war on drugs is working. If you think the money is moved in suitcases, you're watching too many movies. The big drug money is moved through bank transactions.

Not to long ago, Colombia was given six billion dollars to stop the flow of drugs to America, by us, the taxpayers. Hell, I don't even think they slowed it down. I could take those six billion dollars and start an independent company that would use the money for manpower and high-tech surveillance at the borders, airports, and loading docks, which would hamper the flow of drugs tremendously, instead of sending it to some country where most of it ends up in corrupt politicians' pockets.

• The cave dwellers found out there was something to cannabis when they caught their first buzz, sniffing it in a fire. They realized it was similar to the buzz they got from fermented fruit. Most young Americans during the last three decades or more have tried grass at an impressionable age, just like all the other no-nos that are illegal or exciting and you aren't suppose to do. It would also be fair to say that 50 percent of adults have at least tried some sort of drug or another, in that same time period. Source-knowledge came to people from information obtained from the media, movies, and TV, where the whole purpose is to create sensationalism for the viewers. These same people will blame marijuana when a youngster takes the wrong road and ends up in trouble. They don't seem to take into account other contributing factors, such as alcohol, a more powerful drug, or a major factor, the kid's mental status. Who's at fault here, the youngster whose head is messed up because of his environment and probably being raised with no parental supervision, or a drug? The millions of youngsters who don't get all the publicity are the millions who can say "No," been there, done that, and go on with their lives and become solid citizens.

• Inner-city preteens have no control of their situation. Seeing all around them adults who are trying to escape reality by using drugs, they can't help but believe that using drugs is the only way to overcome the pain caused by poverty, disappointment, and resentment. There's a good chance that smoking marijuana will lead them to stronger drugs. But might it also be true that family violence could lead to the making of a killer or that penny-ante stealing could lead to the making of a bank robber?

I'm not implying that marijuana is for everyone; I'm only saying that of all the drugs marijuana is the one to least worry about. People who only smoke pot are not bad people. The ones I know don't go around beating up old ladies or committing brutal crimes. They're not underhanded or lowlifes, like some of the alkies that I have known. These people hold down jobs and take care of their responsibilities and are generally solid individuals. From a bartender's standpoint, I'll take them any day as my customers over the drunks and alcoholics.

There are some adults who get high on weekends to enjoy a night out or attend a concert; they get high in the privacy of their homes with friends. These people use grass to enhance a moment or event, not to hurt anyone. There are adult stone-heads who will smoke themselves into a paranoid state of mind and be afraid to socialize. But, I don't consider these people to be dangerous, either. There will be some do-gooders and so-called upright citizens who would say I'm full of shit. Well, they don't know blue-collar middle-class America, as I do.

Anybody who knows me can testify to the fact I might have smoked an ounce or so in my day and I'm not afraid to admit it (for the record, I inhaled it, too). Marijuana does enlighten me and helps me get a better outlook on life in many ways, and I'm not ashamed about liking it, and if you want to call it a crime, then I guess I'm guilty. I didn't smoke pot until I was in my early thirties; before that, I thought it was one of the worst things you could do. It was shortly after my divorce and I was trying to get rid of my guilty feelings about leaving my children by crawling into a whiskey bottle. I can honestly say I might be dead by now, or close to it, if it weren't for ganja.

Because of the way our complicated brain functions, there will be pros and cons for every kind of stimulant humans desire, like marijuana; for some people, it opens up a part of their brain, allowing them to see things from a completely different perspective. It can be used for creativity by musicians or artists; it can make a good muscle relaxant for aches and pains; it has a calming effect on a person who may be tense or stressed, not unlike a Valium that a doctor may prescribe for you. Marijuana can also have a down side, such as making some people sick or paranoid, or you tired and wanting to crash. But, one thing for sure, I've never seen it responsible for anger or violence.

I can affirm that ganja can make good times better, funny movies funnier, humor more humorous. If you have a willing partner, it can make a good aphrodisiac to elevate sexual pleasure. It is great for enjoying music and can help make you lighter on your feet when dancing. One can have interesting conversations with a group of friends, get the munchies and cook up some tasty food for company and watch them eat the hell out of it. The bottom line is for some people it has a lot of wonderful uses that don't hurt a soul.

• Not too long ago, when in Canada, I was sitting in a coffee house with friends of mine, Rosie and Sharon. We watched as people sat around chitchatting, sipping coffee, and smoking ganja. It wasn't sold there, but it was allowed to be smoked there. I saw nothing wrong with this controlled freedom. I don't want to give the impression that I'm advocating drug use, but I think making marijuana legal would eliminate the desire to do wrong that seems to tempt the young.

• As for amphetamines, my first recollection of speed was while reading about certain athletes, who, at the time, were being accused of taking uppers. In my early twenties I was playing basketball with some of the best players in Toledo; some of the guys were older than I, some were even ex-college players, but they all told how it was common practice for trainers at school to pass out uppers before the games. Back then, it was no big deal for somebody to openly ask if anyone had an upper or a "benny," as they were sometimes called.

A buddy with whom I played basketball used and sold pills to fellow ball players. Because he needed a bigger supply, he asked me to help him out. Thinking nothing of it, I went to see the doctor he used, with instructions on how to go about getting the pills. I was told to tell him I had a weight problem, and I needed diet pills. I walked into his office a little nervous, I told him I was a friend of so and so's, then told him my story. Before I knew it, without an examination and with no more than a look in the eye, the doctor got a big jug, scooped these pills out, and counted out a hundred. I handed him the money and was out the door in five minutes. What was really amazing is that I only weighed 165 pounds at the time!

Thanks to the medical profession and the latest cure-all for weight, in the middle sixties diet pills became the rage. Running to the cupboard for mother's little helper was more than just a lyric in a song.

I remember one time when I had a terrible hangover after a rough night in the bar. Going to work in the morning at the factory was like facing death; I stopped and picked up a friend I worked with. He saw the condition I was in and offered me a diet pill; he said his wife was getting them from their doctor. After he explained how they helped him, and I was feeling so bad that I was desperate, I said "What the hell," and down the hatch it went. Well, I found out why they call it speed. They couldn't have come up with a more fitting name, for not only did I cruise through the workday, but on the way home after work, I felt like I could get out and run alongside the car.

In the late sixties and early seventies bar scene, speed was so common it was like asking for an aspirin. There was always someone looking for a hit and they didn't have to look very hard to find one. There usually was some girl chewing her gum into submission who had a bottle in her purse or a guy who looked like he's been fasting for six years hopping from foot to foot chain smoking. Customers who were on that kind of high drank faster than I could pour 'em, but they never got staggering drunk. They would get edgy with a good possibility of getting mean. If that happened to a man and he started some trouble, more often than not, it would take at least two people to get him out the door. Speed freaks are half-superman, half-contortionist and a whole lot of stupidity. Once people got

used to speed, it wasn't much of a transition to coke, since
both drugs have the same purpose.

• Great men, like leaders, rulers, popes, inventors, scientists, and other innovative people of history mention their
desire for cocaine-based drinks. A pope who was supposed to
be one of the best, Pope Leo VIII, called a cocaine-based
liqueur he indulged in "a benefactor of humanity."

In the early 1900s, America had cocaine-based products
like chewing gum, soda pop, and cigarettes. These items were
sold right along with the over-the-counter cocaine-based medicines. Doctors of the day prescribed cocaine-based medicines
as often as the doctors of today push antibiotics for all our
ailments. After the AMA took control of our lives, cocaine
became an illegal drug, unless you have a prescription.

When coke became a fad in the mid seventies, passed on by
the jet-setters and the Hollywood "in" crowd, without looking
over their shoulder for fear of repercussions, people in bars
that I worked in would brag about having coke on them.
Attention-getters had razors and little spoons hanging around
their necks, wore rings designed for the purpose, and even let
the fingernail on their pinkie grow longer to snort it with. To
me this wasn't so terrible, for these were only adults engaging
in the latest cool thing to do. It had nothing to do with the real
person. At least they didn't stagger out the door and drive, but
most definitely they drove home too fast.

In the beginning, cocaine was called a recreational drug,
and it was basically available only to higher income people.
Then it started gaining popularity and spread to all classes of
people. American business, with its own manipulated version
of free enterprise, saw the money-making opportunity that
coke could provide, the opportunity for importing, manufac-
turing, distributing, and marketing. It was inevitable that,
sooner or later, big business would jump on the bandwagon.

It was also at the same time that they blamed a president
for the big drop in the price of gold. Coke became worth more
than gold. Not only in America, but everywhere your big financiers started putting their money into cocaine. Remember
when they busted that rich stainless-steel car guy in a coke

deal? When was there ever a drug in our modern-day culture, which has a big turnover because of addiction, not controlled by high finance?

Observing customers from my invisible spot behind the bar, I picked up on the different tendencies of each drug. Some that I've noticed about coke are people checking their noses after leaving the john; like speed, it makes people hyper; some get a form of paranoia; and others get geeked and almost dislocate their jaw grinding their teeth. The girls will hang on who's carrying or is a dealer, like flies on shit. For some reason, most of the ladies seem to have a stronger craving for it than men do.

I've had many conversations with both sexes about how coke affects them sexually; men have told me if they do too much they can't get it up and others will say it keeps them going all night long. Women have told me it's a great aphrodisiac, not that women need anything to have sex all night long.

One misconception is that coke gives you all this energy. It does at first, but sooner or later you'll crash hard. Now you've got to have more, because you're so beat. After a while, more is not enough, so you end up with a bad case of cocaine blues and an addiction. Coke is not a good drug. Period. Anyone who has abused it and gets hooked knows better than I do how terrible coke can be. I once heard a comedian say that the first thing he realized after he got off coke was that he had an income.

• When crack cocaine hit the mainstream, I was pretty much out of the bar business, so I never really had the opportunity to experience many crackheads; I guess I was lucky. The only thing I know for sure is that crack is evil. I've never seen or heard anything good come out of using or dealing in it.

The number of deaths due to crack are far worse than deaths related to controlled substances during the Prohibition era. Back then, it was basically adults who were involved in the killing of each other over the control and distribution of alcohol. The difference today is crack cocaine is killing our most valuable assets for the future, young minds. Young people are killing each other, killing someone to get crack, or they O.D. on it before they even have a chance to figure out what life is all about. Killings done by young people weren't this prevalent before crack cocaine became such a big money-making business.

If we used even half of the money that is wasted protecting American conglomerate business interests in a foreign country (which create a country full of people who hate Americans), and put the same kind of effort and expense into solving the problem that leads to crack addiction here in America, not only would we eliminate kids dying because of crack cocaine, we would also be saving thousands of young minds. This is called taking charge of our country's future.

• Heroin is another ugly drug; it's a toss-up between heroin and crack as to which is the greater evil. In my youth, you might have heard stories about heroin users, but hop heads, as they were called, were few and far between. It was a rare occurrence for a heroin addict to come into any of the bars that I worked in, and the few that I did know about never caused any problems. But I always kept one eye on them anyway, just in case. The reason that they don't frequent bars is that, just like an alkie, they spend all their money on their drugs.

When I managed the hotel that I mentioned earlier, I had some bad times with heroin addicts. They can be very scary S.B.s to deal with. In those days, I carried a gun in my back pocket for protection and on more than one occasion I'm glad that I did. One incident that I was involved in got very intense. I had to stop a disturbance in one of the rooms. It was between two gay heroin addicts and one was cutting the other guy up with a razor. When they opened the door and I saw the situation, I sent the desk clerk who was with me to go call the police. After a few minutes of exchanging words about the rules of the hotel, the razor guy flipped out and went ballistic on me. He went into a rage and started waving the razor around, calling me a M.F. and shouting how he was going to cut my white ass. He stepped out into the hall and I backed up and pulled my gun. I told him to settle down and warned him that the police were on their way. He still kept coming and made a lunge at me. I shot him in the leg and he fell down but started crawling toward me with a wild look in his red bloodshot eyes, yelling at me how he was going to kill me. I'm happy to say that the police arrived just in the nick of time.

His reason for violent behavior stems from something in his head, but the drug is the catalyst that fires up that hate and also doesn't allow simple logic to come into play.

Something more disgusting and puzzling was another heroin situation I got hoodwinked into. This event was a real eye-opener. It was in the mid eighties. I met a young girl in the factory where I worked; we went out three or four times and she would spend a weekend with me once in awhile. I got to know her pretty well; anyway I thought I did. One night when I picked her up, she asked me to make a stop where she had to pick something up.

We went to this house in a neighborhood in a bad part of town. She ran up to the house where a middle-aged black woman met her at the door. After a short conversation, she came back to me and said, "We have to go inside for a minute." By then I got the picture. The woman met me at the door with a nervous look, but after the girl explained I worked at the factory with so and so, who was one of the woman's friends and was also a dealer, she relaxed. Before I ever saw the big table surrounded by chairs filled with people, I knew it was a shooting gallery. There were two sleazy-looking colored guys, a young girl besides the one I was with, a couple of white factory workers, and a businessman in an expensive-looking suit. I could tell they were getting nervous about my presence by the stares of the colored guys and the factory workers. There was no eye contact from the businessman. I just happened to have a doobie on me, so I lit it up, to show them I wasn't a narc. It seemed to do the trick and in a few minutes everyone relaxed and there were even a few smiles.

They all sat there waiting for the delivery of their junk, getting jumpier with every sound of a car going by. There was a sound of a car door and everybody perked up right on cue; the woman ran to the window, then turned around and said it was a false alarm. On cue again, they all relaxed at the same time. Well, it finally got there; everybody went into a frenzy getting their rubber bands, spoons, lighters, and needles out. Seeing all of those adults hurrying to stick needles in, draw out blood, then shoot the heroin into their arms and a few other places, was one of the most sickening and frightening things I've ever witnessed. To this day, I can't understand how they could get to that point. Needless to say, I dropped the girl off at some bar with a goodbye. After seeing those adults doing that to themselves because of a drug, how can anyone expect a youngster to have a chance against something that is so habit-forming?

Heroin is back big time. In Toledo (which is one or two years behind the big trend-setting cities), it's being used more by young people from all backgrounds more than it ever was and has elevated up near the top of the illegal street drugs. Years back, it was basically a needle-induced drug; now it's a cool fad. People are snorting heroin along with coke like the big celebrities who are glorified in the entertainment world. Don't think that a few underworld characters who make the news and the dealers in the streets are responsible for such a large distribution of a product where hundreds of millions are involved.

With heroin made available and less expensive than it used to be and marketed like any other hot item, volume and fast turnover result in quick returns. Throw in addiction, and you're talking megabucks. This is big business. You can't move hundreds of millions without going through banks. As I said earlier, it's not done with suitcases. You hear from the media how we can't control it and officials constantly saying that we need more tax dollars for the drug war; but we have the clout to tie up bank assets and business holdings, and put sanctions on a whole country. This is how our double-standard system works when it benefits American government and big business, which is the same thing.

We need to quit pointing fingers at the users and dealers and gain more knowledge of who is really responsible. Only when we target the ones who can obtain the assets for such large distribution and profit and their financial backers, we will be able to stop this terrible plague. This is my view gained through my lifestyle. You don't have to believe it or take it to the bank, but if you don't totally disbelieve and give more thought about banks, I'll be satisfied.

• Hallucinogens, like most drugs, go back centuries. Peyote was used by early cultures for celebrating and providing stamina for fighting battles; witch doctors, Merlins, high priests, whatever they were called, used it for control and mystical powers as a cure-all. I would like to go back in some kind of time machine to see the reaction of a caveman on his first trip, after he stumbled on some magic mushrooms. Maybe that's how they discovered fire or the wheel. Frankly speaking, hallucinogens allow you to see things in a different perspective; they open up parts of the brain that you didn't know were there, and you'll finally see what you've been looking at for ages.

Forms of hallucinogens, like LSD, mescaline, and others, have been called "mind-altering drugs." To most it sounds scary. "Like wow, man," what drug doesn't change our thinking? Where would humans be now if our minds didn't alter?

"Expanding the consciousness" has a good sound to it. It became a popular phrase in the late sixties when it was identified with the psychedelic hippie scene. But long before it was associated with LSD, it has been a puzzling question for philosophers and scientists to theorize on for ages.

LSD got a kick start in the illicit market when the media, movies, and music marketed its usage for sensationalism, such as misleading explanations by the press of Dr. Leary's opinions on its merits, things like people jumping out of windows, movies putting the morality of free love and flower children in a bad light, a person freaking out on acid, the music industry publicizing satanic lyrics and glorifying bands trashing rooms in a hotel and then blaming acid for their stupidity. But we didn't see shit in the press when the CIA used it in mind-altering experiments that resulted in the deaths of human guinea pigs. When the financial system makes a commitment to a product, good or bad, it will happen. Remember when people bought the pet rock?

• For people with strong minds, some drugs can be recreational. For people with weak minds, drugs will only camouflage their troubles, which will still be prowling around in their brain long after the drug wears off.

I do remember the sixties. I was not hating people for their use of drugs then, but I was against drugs. Other than taking speed a couple of times, I was drug-free, as they say today. But I still have the strong conviction that put me down on drugs in the first place: they're bad for young minds. Because my outlook on life has been consistent from then until now, I believe in freedom of choice for adults within reason. For adults who are mad at the world, have a violent nature, or suffer from depression and other mental hang-ups, hallucinogens are bad ju-ju. Youngsters don't need them and should be kept from trying them if at all possible. I wouldn't know how to stop them short of twenty-four-hour surveillance. Who, when they were young, didn't think, "It can't happen to me; I'm invincible and I won't get caught"? I'm sure drugs have been used by teenagers for a long time, but 99 percent of them made it and became responsible adults.

I was thirty-eight the first time I took a trip. It was the blizzard of '78. A girlfriend and I with two other couples were snowed in for three days. We had no alternative but to party. It was suggested we do mushrooms. I was reluctant at first but broke down under the pressure from the five other willing participants. I have not regretted that decision; we laughed until we pissed ourselves and had a hilarious time.

The real plus was I realized how amazing and powerful the brain is. It hit me during a ping-pong match with my buddy. The orange ball had tracers behind it and I just cracked up. All six of us grownups laughed and played like little kids and ate a lot. Every time I hear the blizzard of '78 mentioned, I think of mushrooms. At that time I'd just started reading books about the mind from health to psychology. After experiencing this trip, it gave me a better understanding of the books I read. I couldn't stop thinking about how that minute particle of a mushroom could have such an effect on the brain. That experience and others after that have taught me more about this beautiful mind we have more than any book could have. I'm not saying you should be living there all the time, but it's not a bad place to visit on occasion. Frankly speaking, if you have a good attitude, a good outlook on life, and enjoy great laughter, I don't know of a happier drug.

• The wealthy have usually been the pacesetters in recreational drugs. I found this to be true while tending bar when the so-called drug culture was in full swing. It was inevitable that the dealers would invade suburbia. Having the purchasing power has put the suburbans at the forefront for obtaining the latest drug being marketed by the black market economy. The big numbers needed for big profit in the illicit drug trade come from the youth of suburbia to the inner city.

• I have very little experience with fantasy, ecstasy, date-rape (not the first drug in history to have this distinction), and other synthetic drugs used today. Regardless of my limited knowledge of this new wave of drugs used for the never-ending quest for a different, higher effect, their usage is for the same purpose as that of other drugs: enjoyment, enlightenment, and the reasons that made them so prevalent in today's society, namely overcoming depression, ducking reality, and giving in to temptation.

• The traits of youth have been and always will be the urge to be different from grown-ups, the rebelliousness to do what's not allowed. They are easily influenced and very impressionable. The entertainment industry uses these traits to market sensationalism, glorifying the evils of drugs in movies with the "cool" drugged-out dudes, dames, and dealers, selling to the easily impressionable youth (this also made the industry $$$).

With all the subliminal preprogramming of the young today, one of the best safeguards for parents against losing their child to drugs is, "Don't let them get convinced that being yourself is not good enough."

• Frankly speaking, religion is the strongest drug in the world to get people hating and killing each other over different beliefs and who's god is the best. Now, that's surely a strong drug.

Chapter VIII

SEX

Where else besides in the bedroom is sex on people's minds than in bars and nightsclubs? You have all the components needed for the game of sex: men, women, alcohol, and music. Maybe the neighborhood bars could maintain without it, but nightclubs without sex in the air would be like TV without a picture; there just wouldn't be any.

We all have our weaknesses and, assuredly, sex is mine. Some of my biggest mistakes in life were judgment calls involving sex. When my testosterone got fired up and my libido was in high gear, "Hector" (who lives in my pants) with his little pea brain has occasionally overpowered my other brain, resulting in some sexual encounters that were not pre-meditated acts to hurt someone, but unfortunately they turned out that way. The only drawback to sex worldwide that I see is that we are screwing ourselves out of a future, by extreme overpopulation.

As a bartender, suggestive sex is part of your repertoire. Suggestive sex can get more laughter without offending anyone, more than the cheap shots, such as swearing and vulgarity (like using the F-word), ever will. And I always consider it a lot classier playing on words in regular chitchat with people at the bar or the lyrics of a song on the jukebox using suggestive sex to create humor. It can loosen up new customers and sometimes get a smile out of someone in a bad mood. It is also great in helping break the ice for new relationships with the opposite sex.

Who knows how many people have died in wars throughout history that were fought because of sex and jealousy? The
common people are duped into fighting wars over some
trumped-up reasons because their leaders controlled information. Common folk would fall for it and march off to die.

Death due to jealousy over sex is an ever-occurring event in
America. Bruised egos are also part of the scenario. Adultery
leads to death as much as the desire for power or money does.
Raw emotions fired up by jealousy can make a person commit
regrettable acts of violence and stupidity.

One of the reasons for today's high divorce rate is adultery.
More times than not, the reason behind it can be lack of sex.
As a bartender, I've seen and have been involved with women
who weren't getting any sex at home. So they would come to
bars where their sole purpose is to get laid. For some reason,
there weren't that many men with that problem, or maybe they
just wouldn't admit it to a male bartender.

I don't know if sex is still a part of the marriage ritual in
some circles, but it used to be. To consummate a marriage, sex
was needed. I suspect most people consummate it before
marriage today. I'm a believer in sex before marriage. I think
good lovemaking is an important factor for a long, happy,
loving relationship.

Making up after a fight can mean a trip to the bedroom for
some hot, beautiful sex for most couples. People who have
been together for a while will anticipate a roll in the hay to
make everything all right without any verbal apology necessary!

One-night stands will be around forever, I hope. I know of
cases where they probably saved a marriage or two. Before all
the deadly transmittable diseases popped up, one-night stands
weren't so risky, but today it's a different ballgame, dangerous
and even fatal.

I can't say when or how the bartender sexual mystique got
its start, but I'm quite certain that its promotion in movies,
books, and magazines helped instill it in the woman's libido. It
gave women the idea that we could be had. And they were
right. However the mystique got started, you can be sure it

made the bartender one of the top candidates for one-night stands.

Some single women look for a one-night stand, but most of the women I've had the pleasure to know were married. The major reason for their one-night stands was their husbands no longer gave them the sexual satisfaction that was necessary. Maybe he let himself go and became fat and sloppy? Another reason women have told me is that their love life became routine and mechanical with no variety and excitement.

The reasons married men looking for a one-night stand gave were similar to those of a lot of married women: wives with low self-esteem caused by weight gain don't see themselves as being sexy or even desirable. But a bigger reason is that they quit being a whore in the bedroom. This sends men to the bars for that stimulation that was lost at home. If you think about it, prostitution is a form of a one-night stand.

I'm all for safe sex, just like all level-headed people. Besides the disease factor, overpopulation is the number-one problem facing humans in the future. Something I came across in a book I read awhile back predicted what could happen in the future. You will need a permit to have a child. Frankly, I don't think that's a bad idea for the near future.

Back when venereal diseases didn't kill you, a shot of penicillin did the trick. There was a time when practicing safe sex wasn't that essential, but now one-night stands, even with protection, are like playing Russian roulette.

It's hard enough for adults, but for young people practicing safe sex is a tough thing to do. At the time, doing it feels so good that your mind doesn't think of safety, let alone the consequences. I imagine everyone has been there, and if you haven't, you must still be a virgin.

Well, before the term "safe sex" was ever coined, the birth control pill (a contraceptive) got widespread use across America. At that time, the disease factor wasn't a big issue. The pill was for couples who wanted to enjoy a plentiful sex life without screwing themselves out of a seat at the dinner table. Then it moved quickly into the mainstream, not because couples had too many mouths to feed, but because women, married or not, wanted to have the freedom of a happy sex life without the problems and consequences of getting pregnant.

Some years later, another area where the pill caught on was the concern of parents to make sure that their teens didn't ruin their lives by having children before they had a chance to see what life's all about. Parents allowed and sometimes encouraged their teens to take the pill, knowing it was almost impossible to keep them from having sex, because most remembered that when they were at that age their hormones were going wild and everything else seemed secondary.

The American Medical Association had the medical profession distribute the pill randomly without caring about the long-term side effects it had on women's health. As usual, to the AMA, making money was more important than people's health. Most people have the false conception that the AMA is an organization run by medical-minded people. In reality, the AMA is made up of heads of businesses, drug companies, and board members of financial institutions.

At the time, they didn't tell you about the harmful consequences of taking the birth control pill. Drugs advertised on TV today warn that you may suffer one or more of these side effects, such as nausea, dizziness, drop in sex life, diarrhea, heart problems and high blood pressure, liver damage, limp dick, etc. For the last thirty years or more, 50 percent of cancers women are being treated for (or have died from) are the result of the pill. Besides reading about the cancers and other female problems the pill is responsible for, I have personally known several women who have had serious health problems caused by the pill.

Contraceptives primarily have been the responsibility of the woman. For the man it's "Slam, bam, thank you ma'am!" without worrying about complications of getting pregnant women are faced with, for instance, the caring and welfare of a baby, not to mention watching your body swell out of proportion for the painful event. It's a heavy price to pay for a quick roll in the hay. Very few men think of the consequences or the obligations that result when hormones take over the brain.

One reason men were not part of the medical view on contraceptives is that throughout history it's been a man's world. Not until recently has the woman's opinion carried any weight in any major decision-making in America. I read articles in science and medical books, and also in magazines, years ago about the patch on the arm and the pill for men. Why it was not imperative to distribute them to men, only the powers that be can answer that question. I guess it goes back to the old saying, "It's a man's world."

If the male contraceptive had been in use as long as the woman's has, some of the social ills of the inner city wouldn't be so devastating. To start with, there wouldn't be so many children growing up not knowing or having a father. The cost of welfare for the taxpayer would be cut dramatically. The overcrowded conditions that create poverty, violence, and crime would be less of a problem, and most importantly, you wouldn't have the lives of millions of teens getting off to a bad start with only a bleak and scary outlook for the future.

There was a hit song out not too long ago with the lyrics, "Who let the dogs out?" It referred to the inner-city male youth who go around screwing girls without the worry or responsibility for the consequences, just like dogs in the street do. That shouldn't be the mindset of the inner-city youth.

A strong, healthy sex drive can be a curse. I knew myself well enough that after my divorce, because of my love for the opposite sex, I made sure I had a built-in contraceptive (I got a vasectomy in 1970). As the years went by, it turned out to be very beneficial for me. A lot of women were more than willing to have sex with me because of not having to worry about getting pregnant. It also saved me from a different kind of problem a man in my position faced. I was dating a certain girl off and on for four or five months; then I didn't go out with her or see her for awhile. One night, she came into the bar while I was working; she had a long, sad face and she wasn't saying very much. When I started talking to her, she explained to me that we had a problem. She told me that she was pregnant, and that I was the father. Well, I told her about my vasectomy; she got all red-faced and out the door she went. I never saw her again.

When I was growing up, if you got to see the flesh on the thigh right above the nylon on a woman, you would get quite a thrill. Then, in the late sixties, the minidress, which was just a tad away from the touch-me-not, became popular and very uplifting to men. But since then, women displaying themselves sexually goes way beyond their dress.

Women nowadays express their desires and intentions about sex openly in conversations with men present, without caring if it sounds trashy or slutty. It used to be, such conduct wasn't ladylike, but gone are those days. Good girls get married, bad girls have fun is a reality more now than it ever was. But there are a lot of men who still think that the feminine side of a woman shows class.

The no-bra look was, and still is, cool. Now the rage is wearing a sheer bra that highlights the nipple, which is just as stimulating. Either way, it's sexy and not outright trampy. Now, just to get noticed, girls tend to be obscene and easy. If you have a string of beads or just ask, girls are more than willing to show you nipple and all. I've been in nightclubs lately where girls will get up at eye level whether on stage or tables and want you to see that they're wearing a thong or no panties at all, leaving nothing to the imagination. I guess I'm old-fashioned, but being sexy should be a natural characteristic, without flaunting a cheap outer shine.

There's one aspect about sex in the new millennium that's missing: the chase. In most cases today, sex is predetermined before the first date: "Don't forget to bring the condoms." There were a few girls in my neighborhood when I was a teenager who put out. (For some reason, they all were Polish-Catholic girls. When my buddy and I got older we used to laugh about the coincidence.) But unless you were somebody special (like a high-school athlete), good-looking, or had a cool car, your chances of getting laid were next to none, without a lengthy dating procedure.

In my day, when a guy would take a girl to the movies, after buying her popcorn and candy, he might get the chance to put his arm around her shoulder. By the end of the first feature (if his arm didn't fall asleep), he might be lucky enough to get his hand to the top of her boob, and man, he was in seventh heaven! There seemed to be more self-respect back then. The youths of the new millennium don't seem to have respect for much of anything, let alone for themselves. It's more important for them to be cool and follow the crowd.

When the massage vibrator went from massaging the shoulders and back to the breast and crack, lovemaking between a man and a woman wasn't always necessary for sexual gratification.

Today's women like showing their sexual freedom in various ways. One of the latest ways is the sex toy party. These parties make Tupperware parties seem a bit boring, but I'm sure they're still keeping the plastic industry happy.

I picked up a lady friend of mine who was at one of these sex toy parties not too long ago. When I got there, the main show was over, but I got a chance to see some of the props still on display. What I saw would make the average man feel inadequate, or at least want to try a lot harder with more imagination in sex. I know girls will be girls, but some of those "toys" looked pretty scary to me.

I think a dildo can be a helping hand for some women; they can be a replacement for a real man, when none are beating down your door, especially when you're not wanting to get involved in a relationship at the present time, but still wanting a little sexual relief. Sex toys can become a fantasy lover, the need for the bigger things in life to produce multiple orgasms, which some women find essential or hard to obtain. Years ago, I was in a threesome with my girlfriend and Bruno. Bruno was her friend she kept in the drawer next to the bed. I had no problem with it. I know some women need more than a guy can give on occasion.

I think sexual fulfillment should be at everyone's fingertips. But some women I know want the whole package, the soft lips, the tender touch of the hands, the soft words, and the rest of the things a man does to a woman so she can have that climactic moment. Frankly, it takes two to tango.

Most men like the real thing, that beautiful, warm little beaver. But there are a few weirdos who are not satisfied with

Nancy palm and Susie five fingers, and buy themselves a plastic vagina for their sexual pleasure. I really do feel sorry for any man who is in that situation.

When it comes to sales, the one-size-fits-all plastic beavers can't compare to the dildos being purchased by women. I know there are more women on earth than men, but I think it would be fair to say that's not the only reason for the dildo's higher sales advantage. For one thing, women are adjustable.

I don't know if most women understand that men have to get blood to old woody for performance. Men can't just lie there like some women do, with legs spread apart, asking, "What's wrong with you?"

Men, why should you let a piece of plastic keep you from having a good relationship? (If the size of the penis is the only hiccup in a marriage, off to the sex shop, not the divorce court.)

Most men, when they think of love, really think of sex. When women think of sex, most think of love. I mentioned earlier about me, the bartender, being a shrink without a couch. The one conversation that came up more than any other would be that of a woman telling me the most intimate things in her private life. And nine out of ten times, it was about the lack of adequacy and fulfillment in her sex life. How the main man in her life, a husband, ex-husband, steady boyfriend, or just men in general that she has dated, didn't perform well between the sheets. What it boiled down to is that the men didn't make love; all they did was fuck. I guess that's why they were sitting in the bar telling me; they weren't fortunate enough to have a man who is a romantic. Being a romantic myself, I know; sex is like life, it's all about giving.

Not too long ago, unlike today, explicit and detailed information on sex wasn't readily available for young people. Most parents were still doing it missionary style, and oral sex wasn't indulged in like in today's society. The mindset on sex in most families was: You weren't supposed to talk about sex and if it was discussed, it was done in a discreet manner. Mostly due to traditionally acquired beliefs (or our Christian training), there was one and only one view on sex. A lot of men thought that after they climaxed their job was done and that the erogenous zone was someplace on a world map. If a woman wanted more sex and creative lovemaking, then she must be a whore.

I have talked to a few men who have said it was the other way around; they had wives who would just lie there and wouldn't even undress in front of them unless the lights were out. These were the men who ended up with mistresses or paid for uninhibited sex. But most men wouldn't talk about their sex life at home, pro or con (not to a male bartender, anyway).

To say that past generations were wrong about their knowledge of the pleasure of sex wouldn't be fair. If you go back twenty-five years, people were pressured into getting married at a young age and most young people were inexperienced in lovemaking. The parents would encourage their children to hurry up and get married, have a family, and take on all the responsibility just like they did right after high school (unless you were able to go to college). If you were in your early to middle twenties and still at home, you would be an embarrassment to the family.

Movies, TV, porn on the Internet, all the reading material that's available, and sex education taught in school, have made today's young people's quest for sexual awareness more important than the knowledge you need to handle it. I wish our society was committed to teaching kids about life's pitfalls, the strength of education, and the reality of adulthood, with the same exuberance and financial backing that we put forth in marketing sensationalism. Millions of young adults would be happy, healthy, and proud when they become grandparents. It would be asinine to think this marketing shit can be stopped overnight, but if we don't start giving it some serious thought, it won't get any better but will surely get worse. Frankly speaking, I wish the selling point wasn't the point.

We have gone from one extreme to the other in too short a time. Simply think of the movie industry's weak and tasteless way of presenting entertainment by making commercials that are nothing but subliminal ways of using sex sensationalism, like porking an apple pie or having a young girl's head in some boy's crotch. Music videos that have scenes of drive-by shootings and, again, of a girl's head in a boy's crotch, are commonplace. Most favored by kids, and available anywhere, are video games with people lopping each other's heads off, or killing babies. Girls not old enough to drive are partying on the beach with all their goodies hanging out. No wonder Florida leads the nation in rapes. Parents have to draw the line somewhere. I'm not just talking about sex. I'm only asking, when is young too young? To me, it seems like parents have forsaken their responsibilities in the raising of their children.

(There used to be a saying, "A kiss on the lips is a friendly persuasion for an attempt to make a lower invasion." Today the kiss is not necessary.)

Sex is like a science; while doing your research, don't be afraid to experiment. The last moment of a sexual encounter is like the end of anything; it's over. But when the prelude was as pleasurable as the end result, the passionate feeling between two people can be never-ending.

For adults of any age, sex is one of the pleasures that there is in life. It's like eating good food; nobody and nothing can take away the personal enjoyment you get out of it, like having a woman's body pressed against you in a warm hug, then releasing your arms and letting your hands slide along her side with your palms feeling her breasts, then your finger-tips slip over the nipples. I can't speak for her, but for me it's such an enjoyable sensation. A sensation that I don't ever want to lose.

Making love, whether you are in love or not, is the desire to make someone happy by giving your all. Here are some of the things that I have found to be successful and rewarding for both parties:

• The touch, tingle, and tease of soft, lasting foreplay.
• The massage with oil and cream, which stimulates the body and enhances the joy of sex.
• The tender words of inspiration and praise.
• The long, deep, sensual kiss.

• The uninhibited fantasy games that allow the brain to create.

• The self-gratification one gets in pleasing someone with oral sex.

• The arousing effect of being exciting and unpredictable; doing whatever it takes to accomplish a satisfying conclusion in the enjoyment of sex.

In the act of making love, oral sex to some people is like the opening act of a beautiful play. It sets the tone for the rest of the show so you can enjoy the climactic ending.

There have always been women who enjoy the pleasure of giving head, but it wasn't so blatantly done as it is today. You can receive oral sex as a favor, or as a payment for something, like drugs. Maybe to show your feelings for a special someone because it was that time of month. And for some, just to enjoy the old 69 thing.

Oral sex is quite easily obtained now. It doesn't seem to have the value that it used to have, when it used to be far and few between. Performing oral sex today is as common to young people as a French kiss used to be years ago. Young girls think giving head is the cool thing to do. B.J.s have turned into a necessity for bragging rights, instead of being a symbol of passion.

It used to be that black women didn't like to perform oral sex. Some of my black friends would tell me that the reason they hit on white women was to get some head, because their women at home wouldn't perform oral sex. I believe that has changed through the years; I hope it has, for my friend's sake.

Anal sex, like any other form of sex, is a matter of personal preference, just as long as no one gets hurt and you both enjoy it; that's called freedom. But it's all Greek to me and it can get you in a crappy situation.

Some women (for reasons unknown to me) are ready and willing to have sex with any man with a status symbol, such as a bartender, a band member, an athlete, or a man in a uniform. I suspect that they are taken in by the celebrity aura of these people. It's a wanting that most women will not display for the ordinary run-of-the mill guy.

I've experienced first-hand how women would react to me differently when I was a customer than when I was their bartender. I would be drinking on my night off in the bar that I worked in and strike up a conversation with a woman who just happened to be there for the first time. Sometimes she would brush me off politely, or hint that she was not attracted to me, and I didn't have a chance with her. If she came in the next night while I was working, she couldn't wait to get my attention, hanging over the bar with a big smile and a cleavage shot to go with it, yelling, "Oh Frank, oh Frank!"

In 1983, long before that crocodile bloke from Australia made the scene, I went on a sailing trip on Lake Michigan with my friend John to Saugatuck, Michigan on the Black River, a resort where they have a big Fourth of July holiday bash. Whenever I sailed with Captain John on his boat, I would have fun with people whenever they were within earshot of us, hamming it up by using a mixture of Aussie and old pirate-movie lingo. After arriving and making everything shipshape, we hit the clubs. At this one place, while we were having a drink and conversation, I started to ham it up with my phony Aussie accent. Sitting next to John were two women who heard me talking and asked John where I was from. Well, John jumped on this opportunity to have some fun. He told them I was his friend from Down Under who was visiting him. For two days and nights, all four of us partied on John's boat and in clubs, without this girl ever leaving my side and my faking this accent the whole time.

After a couple of days of being invited to parties on these big expensive boats of Chicago's wealthy and mingling with people treating me like some kind of celebrity (because they thought I was from Down Under and the women were eager to hear me talk with that fake Aussie accent), I got tired of playing the role.

The second night I was with this girl, I looked at her and said, "I can't keep this up any longer; I'm an American." Before

I could explain to her that it was just innocent fun we got carried away with, she was gone.

Because we never had a chance to discuss the situation, I can only assume by her reaction that she was embarrassed. (I was expecting her to be angry.) Just by the look on her face, I think she felt bad about falling for the accent, not the person.

Frankly speaking, one's sexual preference is a personal privilege and as long as your sex habits don't hurt anyone, GO FOR IT!

Two passions, both fulfilling and fun,
Smiling, breathing hard and wringing wet,
In pleasure full circle I've come
From satisfaction received in sports and sex.

Chapter IX

SPORTS

Besides sex, sports is a topic about which a bartender has up-to-date information. Any bartender can tell you that conversation dealing with sports is a big part of the bar environment. A bartender can be on top of the sports scene without having to read a newspaper or see sports news on TV. If a bartender doesn't know the latest trades or the latest score of the big game, and let's not forget the big fight that they always start the TV sports news with (and I'm not talking about boxing), it wouldn't take long for one of the customers to fill him in.

Bars and sports are both associated with recreation for adults in America. I knew a lot of people who went to bars for recreation. Some went for a bar's sporting games or an outdoor recreational activity associated with the bar. And some others went for the recreational activity of exercising the elbow.

Most of the neighborhood bars I grew up in were sports oriented. They sponsored softball and baseball, bowling teams, and other sports of that category. But I would say that all of them had what I call "bar sporting games" as part of their draw, such as pool, gaming machines, cards, betting pools, and darts. The kinds of darts I'm talking about are not the sissy English darts. I'm talking about six inches of wood and feathers with a steel tip that you have to throw twenty-five feet. It's among the most competitive bar sporting games I have ever played.

Sports in neighborhood bars were there to bring in some extra revenue, but weren't the main attraction. People who were on one of the bar's teams or leagues would fulfill an obligation to the owner to stop in and have a drink, whether it was game night or not. After the games, 70 percent of the players along with friends of the team that the bar sponsored would usually come in. Even if you weren't a big drinker, it was a way to say "thank you" to the owner. And if you won, you could always count on a free round. Sports were to help support the business; it wasn't until many years later that "sports bars" became a business.

Today, bars and sports are the bookends for a major industry. Seeing the marketing potential of sports in bars, the business world couldn't pass up the chance to get monetarily involved, creating a network of businesses that revolved around sports and made sports bars a part of the nightlife recreation menu.

The beneficiaries are breweries and beverage distributors, who are the recipients of more sales. Other big lumps of money that sports bars generate are TV viewing time; cable and satellite TV revenue; money made on sports bar franchises; sales of hats, clothing, logos, and other paraphernalia, and so on. Agents and lawyers get a piece of the action, and to top it all off, there is the government's cut. All of these add up to a major industry. Today a bar with one TV is about as obsolete as a bank without a drive-thru window.

Every day, psychology shows you that changes are a big part of growing up. Young people don't want to do things the same as the generation before them. They want to wear a different style of clothes, get into new fads, find new hangouts and rub elbows with new people. Marketing is psychology, and its main goal is to create new outlets for the next generation's spending.

When Joe the customer walks into the bar, he says, "Hi there, *Sport*." I say, "Good evening, that's a *sporty* looking jacket you're wearing tonight, Joe." I ask a customer to please move down one stool so Joe can sit in his favorite spot. Joe tells the customer, "Thank you, you're a good *sport*." As I'm mixing Joe's cocktail, he bets me a drink that what I mix in the shaker won't stop at the rim of the glass. I say, "Okay, I'll be a *sport* about it." I tell Joe I'm pretty good at this, but he has a *sporting* chance. I was close but a dribble too much, and I conceded. Joe thanked me and said, "That's mighty *sporting* of you."

Sports are a reflection of what's wrong with people in today's lifestyle. Everybody has to be Number One to feel like he's somebody. No one plays for the love of the game. Being Number One is more important than the team in the game of life. Just like road rage, everyone is in a hurry to be first, but down the road you will still have to wait your turn. Since the fifties, when sports hit millions of homes through TV and touched millions of people, sports have rearranged our priorities. Loyalty is determined by how many zeroes follow the first number on your paycheck. It's out of control; life is all about money, and it doesn't make any sense to me.

Being Number Two isn't good enough anymore: College coaches are fired because of losing the big game, after doing a terrific job, having a winning history, and a winning season. How does this instill sportsmanship and fair play in the young?

When the dollar signs go off in the board of trustees' greed-induced minds, all they care about is what they might lose in TV contracts, the profit in marketing merchandise, and the rest of the money end of the business. They're not satisfied with what they have gained; the only thing in their heads is the money lost by not being Number One. A college that has a coach like the one I mentioned earlier and a program that's strong can't be losing money. They're just greedy and don't give a shit about sports.

The business, instead of sports, mindset takes a person who works to mould young athletes into a team, teaching them character, among other good principles for adult life, and fires him with no regard or even a speck of human compassion for his feelings, pride, and livelihood, not to mention the embarrassment his family has to endure, because he lost the big game. That preprograms young students to think that loyalty and integrity gained by principles don't mean a thing compared to the profit made in being Number One. To be frank about it, when sports becomes a business, the meaning of sportsmanship is secondary to mo' money.

Very well-paid college administrators eliminate athletic programs that can't be marketed into profit, not caring about how helpful the programs are to young people who obtain scholarships for the education that they wouldn't be able to afford otherwise.

At the same time the administrators are claiming that they don't have the money for sports programs, they make sure they got a raise in pay. The administrators of a college will pay our ex-presidents and other politicians, along with other so-called motivational speakers, heavy sums for speaking engagements. Also there's revenue in the rising prices of tuition, books, dorms, parking, whatever else students need. Yet, we constantly hear the lame excuse, "We don't have the money in our budget." Why don't they have the balls to admit that young people's education doesn't have the importance that profit has?

The same is true with the pros. Coaches who have to deal with multi-million-dollar athletes (spoiled because they're the marketing money-makers who don't play for the love of the game or the team) get fired. All that's important to such athletes are the special contracts their agents deliver, along with the extra perks. Also a coach has to put up with the millionaire owners (or board members) who never played the sport at a high competitive level, but meddle in the running of the team. The owners use the coach as a scapegoat, and fire him when their team finishes second, even though he did the best he could with what he had to work with.

A professional coach got fired a few years ago in the middle of the season when his team was in second place, a few games behind a team that was the defending world champ with a million-dollar roster. I don't want to mention the team, but the socks they wear are red. There's nothing sporting about that.

If firing is to be determined by performance, why do CEOs, politicians, and board members of financial institutions who get caught lying, stealing, and committing fraud, people who make major mistakes that cost the people they're supposed to be working for, not end up paying the price for their mistakes, but keep their jobs? While a person who was doing the best he can gets fired, how do you expect young people, the workforce of the future, to have the incentive to be honest, honorable, and dedicated? Frankly speaking, fans and consumers are the ones paying for the team to be Number One.

• TV is why sports have gone from being a sporting event to an entertainment business. Because of TV contracts, the real competition is between lawyers, agents, and executives, and making money is the only sport. In the movie *North Dallas 40*, the ex-football player turned movie actor gets pissed off, grabs a coach by the collar, and yells at him, "When we call it a game, you call it a business. When we call it a business, you call it a game."

Everyone sits in front of the TV at home and in bars, and bitches about all the money paid to athletes. If you know anything about economics, it's clear that for an athlete to be paid that much money, somebody or some organization has to be making lots more. I don't blame the athletes or hold it against them for the big money they are paid. If it was your child, wouldn't you say, "Take the money and run, kid"? Quit being jealous and think about it.

The headlines in the media about the megabucks that athletes are making are not the whole truth. When agents, lawyers, the league, the team, and Uncle Sam get done, it's still a lot of money, but quite a few other people are padding their pockets with a cut of it. The jock ends up being the fall guy. The problem I have with a lot of the athletes of today is not the money they're making. It's all the attention they want for just doing their job, a very well paid job at that.

• In all my years of watching sports, I've never seen such a bunch of so-called superstars making routine plays that the announcers call "fantastic" or "the greatest ever." If it were just the announcers using these empty phrases, it wouldn't be so bad, but these superstars *believe* they are spectacular. They forget about the three they just dropped.

Catch the ball first, then think about holding your finger up to be Number One or high-fiving and watching yourself on the replay screen. Another thing I don't understand is what or who are they thinking about when they high-five or hold the Number One sign up and do some silly dance when they're *losing*?

• I know why the announcer glorifies a cheap shot for the wannabe fans, but how the hell does an athlete, when he just sucker-punched someone when they didn't see it coming, think he's "the man"? Maybe it was the announcer calling it the defensive play of the game. Frankly speaking, that Number One finger thing should be after the game, when you win.

A good hit is part of the game. But there are too many peewee, grade-school and even high-school coaches who never made it big or even played the sport; most of them are wannabes. Coaches teaching and praising cheap shots was one of the biggest reasons I quit coaching grade-school football.

Coaches forget that one of the most important things they're supposed to be doing is teaching kids sportsmanship. I wonder if they ever take the time to think about what they're doing. Are they aware that a young kid's life can be ruined by these cheap shots? When I coached, I always thought of my love for my son, and I never wanted him, or any other kid, to be paralyzed or killed by a cheap shot. Leave the cheap shots to the pros, where men earning a living get a bonus for it.

• I play volleyball with a bunch of friends who are younger than I. Because I never believed in running across the court to high-five on every good play, I would pass it to them, like blowing a kiss to someone. I would slap my right hand on top of my left while sliding in the players' direction. It saved me a lot of legwork. It would also save a lot of that valuable TV time in sports if the athletes at college and pro levels would adopt it—just a view.

• High-profile athletes who commit crimes make front-page news, but if Joe Dokes commits the same crime, you might read about it on the ninth page of the second section of the paper. The high-profile jock with all the financial clout at his fingertips can hire Berg, Berg, Jones, and Associates, while

Joe Dokes gets a third-string public defender appointed to his case.

When Mr. All-American, who was a role model last year, gets involved in a drug or rape case, or is accused of murder, the media will turn on him and attack like sharks on a kill. Even if proven innocent, after all the accusations and innuendos from the bad press, his reputation, maybe his career, could be ruined.

If it's murder, the case and trial will be the number-one news story everyday, with all the sensationalism the media can pack into it. People get killed every day. But to market news, the media will make this role model a sacrificial goat for all athletes and knock him off the pedestal the media put him on last year. People forget that these role models are just human beings that the media moved from page nine, second section, to the front page. A person who went from Hamburger Helper to surf 'n' turf still has the inner-city mindset embedded in him. The media screw us into the ground with sensationalism, and we're still falling for it. Quit being preprogrammed and make your own judgment; don't just swallow the media judgments.

• "Role model" is a term that was contrived for marketing use. "Role model" wasn't in vogue when I was young, and I know I didn't have one, even though I was as much of an athlete as anybody I knew. There were athletes that I admired as great ball players, but I don't remember idolizing them. I find fault with a young person who chooses as a role model somebody from a TV screen, book, magazine, or newspaper. That role model is not someone the young person comes in contact with, sits down and talks to, and gets to know personally.

• The role models of today are using their names to market overpriced products that kids, under peer pressure, feel they have to wear or have in order to be somebody. And parents who can't afford it pay big bucks for products the basketball player promotes and kids see on TV, with his tongue hanging out, on a drive to the hoop in his famous shoes—the ones that cost a company $10.00 to make (using Third World cheap labor), but end up costing $150.00, after the role-model athlete uses his name to market the product.

The athlete role model who doesn't show the kind of loyalty or principles and bounces from team to team and goes wherever the money is, I see as a good athlete, using his business head and his athletic ability to make money. I don't consider him a role model. A couple of years ago, I saw one of these role models spit in an umpire's face—not too cool of a role model.

• When it comes to the hype in marketing sports, it's nowhere more evident than in announcers. The announcer squeezes his nuts to get a high pitch in his voice to create excitement when he is describing a routine play as spectacular. Announcers preprogram the onlookers by telling them what they're seeing and how they should feel, in order to help ratings that keep their jobs secure. They hype up the latest big star that they're told to market, with statements like, "He's the best who ever played his position," "No one else can make that move," and so on.

The athletes who draw all the media attention are the ones with the best agents, the ones who get the superstars the fat contracts. In their contracts are clauses that guarantee a cut of the money for the league, team, and TV when his name is marketed. This goes right down to the refs making sure the superstar is protected and gets the favorable calls, and coaches who have to make sure the superstar gets a lot of playing time, no matter how he is playing.

The biggest share of sports newscasters and announcers are armchair quarterbacks, wannabes, yes-men who have writers who after editing the tapes come up with snappy catch phrases, which they read off a TelePrompTer, acting like it's spontaneous. Their job is to create an entertainment event, instead of being an announcer at a sporting event.

And when they're not using their written help, they use remarks like "awesome, baby," when a seven-footer stands on his tippy-toes and drops a basketball through a hoop; "fantastic catch," when it was a routine play that thousands of athletes have made; and even call a cheap shot the play of the game. An ex-ballplayer and a real fan who's knowledgeable about the game doesn't have to hear some announcer scream at the top of his lungs to know if it was a fantastic play or not.

• Hockey announcers are probably the most knowledgeable of the major sports, and use their theatrical technique with more style than other major sports announcers. Frankly, they deserve an Emmy just for pronouncing the tongue-twister names so easily.

• Then there are the sick, fanatical fans, most of whom are a bunch of followers and wannabes who never played the sport or are not even knowledgeable about sports, who want to throw beer and scream and fight with an athlete or official. Because of their own dismal lives, and their own disappointment, they actually take things personally, not realizing or accepting that the sports professional is human, and can make a mistake.

Fans who want to fight with a professional athlete have got to have a screw loose. Are they *that* caught up in the frenzy that they think they can hurt a professional athlete? For sure, they have an identity problem—or they think because they paid for a ticket, that gives them the right to be stupid and violent.

I worked in a bar back in the seventies where the players from Toledo's professional hockey team would stop in once in a while. On occasion, some pea brain, for some ungodly reason, would pick a fight with one of these players. I would try to discourage them or settle them down, or the hockey player would try to back off. If that didn't work, I would tell them, "If you're that determined to make a fool of yourself, take it outside." Nine out of ten times, the hockey player would be back through the door before I could serve the next drink.

• Another occurrence that's a mind-blower is the overzealous fans. Whether their team won or lost the big game, they want to tip over, burn something up, riot in the street with the possibility of getting hit over the head with a nightstick, or end up in jail. These fools think it's cool to go to the extreme, instead of being satisfied with celebrating.

One of the sickest things I've seen American fans do lately was boo the Canadian national anthem at a hockey game, because of the behavior of a couple of athletes.

Fans who boo an athlete because of one bad game show their ignorance and lack of discipline in everyday life. There are the brain-dead fans who jump on the bandwagon and go with the media hype wherever it takes them, because of their own inadequacy and knowing nothing about competition or sportsmanship. They live in la-la land, thinking everybody can be Number One. I'm expecting to see the old thumbs-down sign any day now. Sick? Yes. To me, most of the fans today are sick; if we don't start using good old common sense, roller-ball is just around the corner.

• There're not many of the major sports that aren't contaminated by TV hype and money. Football and basketball are so influenced by TV that they have no credibility or luster left in them for me. Football and basketball are so controlled, all you have to do is watch the last two minutes of a game (which usually takes fifteen minutes) to know the results. I'm not trying to sound like a bad sport about this. But it's a view based on my own personal experience.

I've been a football fan for fifty years, played and coached for more than twenty years. And as a bartender, I've been able to hear all the different scenarios on this subject. I ask you this: When you have your opposition down, do you change your defense so the other team can gain confidence and let their offense get a rhythm going? It would be like a company changing a profitable system to give its competition a chance to close the gap.

It was in the late sixties that I first noticed how both TV and gambling syndicates profited by controlling the final minutes and the outcome of the game. At that time, I was involved with a football lottery and handled the tickets for a family in Toledo. About that time, minuses started being used on the football tickets, and prevent defenses in the last two minutes of a game started being used. Minus on a football ticket means that the closer the score at the end of the game, the odds favored the bookies. Also, with the game up for grabs in the final two minutes, everybody is kept glued to the TV. This allows for more commercials and more products to be marketed and brings more money into the TV executives' pockets. Because of blowouts, early football broadcasting executives found out they couldn't market the end of a game as easily as the first part of a game. Since all this has taken place, the rules of the game are changed to accommodate these factors, right down to the TV time-outs.

• Hockey hasn't gotten to the point of the three major sports I mentioned, but it's starting to show the signs of TV control. Hockey players are some of the most skilled athletes in sports. The game of hockey has fast, skillful plays with end-to-end action. But TV sports newscasts will show a fight or some cheap-shot hit for sensationalism before a good scoring play, knowing that will draw the viewers' blood lust and enhance their all-important ratings.

Because of TV selling time for commercials, programming has to be controlled down to the second, making marketing more important than the sport itself. TV executives are changing the way the game is played in order to fit into a fixed timeslot for the benefit of TV scheduling.

From coach of the year getting fired because the million-dollar players didn't produce, or the team being last in the first round of the playoffs, greedy owners say to hell with the feelings of the person doing a good job and axe him because they didn't make enough profit from TV playoff money.

On CBC, an ex-player and coach I consider one of the most knowledgeable and by far one of the most colorful hockey announcers in the game calls it like it is. He refuses American big TV money because of the control of the American TV executives who wouldn't let him speak freely. They're afraid he'll speak out about how American TV is screwing up the game.

The young, new players are the reason the future of hockey will be like that of all the other major sports. The players coming into the game are taught to take cheap shots at opponents when they're not looking. They get congratulated for taking out a good player on the other team, whether fairly or not. They know this will get them on the sports news highlight films and then his agent can get him "mo' money," because that's what TV markets to the fans of today, not the skill of the sport.

How come they can control players leaving the bench when there are fights going on in hockey, while they can't stop bench-clearing brawls in baseball, basketball, and football? Hockey made that rule before TV influenced the sport; that's why the other three sports use all the sensationalism they can to market. My buddy Rosie has three TVs in his family room. We found out you can watch any sport on all three TVs when they're on at the same time, except three hockey pucks.

• Golf is the hardest sport there is to conquer. It's not like team sports where one of your fellow players can bail you out, or you have a bad game but your team wins, or your opposition is having a worse day than you are. Unless you play golf, you can't realize how mental it is.

I played golf for 35 years, and I know the skills involved and the self-discipline it takes. Golf is one of the most gratifying sports there is. It's the most individual sport out there. And as in life, you can't always be at your best; that's why no one athlete can win all the time. In golf, you're dealing with bio-rhythms; sometimes they're up and other times they're down.

Because of money generated for agents, TV, marketing, and media sales, when a player is on top, they get everybody on the money bandwagon. But when a Tiger can't be king of the links all the time, the media turns on him, and call it "choking" to create news, forgetting he's human and sometimes might not win. The media, with its double standards and lust for controversy, calls a player the greatest when he wins, and a choker when he loses. How many athletes can hold it together for four days in a row mentally while competing against the best?

Golf has an oddity that I've never seen in any other sport. In other sports, if an athlete doesn't win anymore, usually he gets booed and then forgotten. Golf fans, though, being knowledgeable and intelligent and having a better appreciation of greatness, know not everyone can be Number One, and nobody can be Number One all the time. Golf has a star who hasn't been a winner for years, but his army is still with him after 50 years; proud to say, I'm one.

There's no sport with the integrity and honesty of pro golfers. They show more class than any other sport out there. They don't badmouth the player who just beat them. They don't scream at officials. They govern themselves and don't cheat. They know what sportsmanship is all about. If countries of the world got along as well as players of different nationalities do in golf, the world wouldn't be in such a mess as it is now.

• Soccer is a sport I never played, and to tell you the truth, I don't know a lot about it. When I was young, this sport was not played in the neighborhood and most of us thought of it as too soft and not a rough, grab-ass sport, which we enjoyed.

As I got older, I appreciated the skill and the great condition of the soccer player, but I still can't get too enthusiastic about it. My granddaughters play soccer, and I love to watch their games. I think it's a great sport for kids. Besides not being violent (at that level), it gives them a chance to play a team sport and gives them an opportunity to get a feeling of teamwork, which will be beneficial to them later in life.

Frankly, I think kids who get a chance to play a team sport, whether they're good or not, will adapt more easily in the workplace later in life. (The opportunity to compete has more importance than winning or losing.) Soccer probably is the most popular sport in the world and has some of the biggest rivalries. When it does get top billing on the American sports news, it's because of riots and deaths that it creates in countries that use this sport for exploitation of political and ethnic differences.

The popularity of soccer is growing in America due to more TV coverage. But when the TV marketing system gets done with it, they will do whatever it takes to make the sport seem more violent, so they can sell it to the violence-oriented American fan.

• Lacrosse is a great sport with a historical background. The skills of the athletes are top-notch and it will have a great future. Lacrosse has all the elements for TV marketing, except excessive violence. But TV influence and the mean nature of today's young athletes will change that. It's a sport I wish I could have played, but in North Toledo, the only pole with a net on it was used for fishing.

• Auto racing? To be frank about it, I don't know much about racing cars. When I was at the driving age, I was all jock and spent my time on a ball field or court, not under the hood of a car. My best friend Bill was a car enthusiast, and if I had a car problem he would bail me out. I always thought Bill should have been a professional racecar driver. He drove hard, but he saved our butts numerous times with his driving skills.

What they have done with marketing auto racing is phenomenal. With all the different camera angles, you feel like you're on the track and in the car. With the in-depth view of technology, it's a big help for a layman like myself. This has helped make it more interesting for me and a lot of other people who didn't enjoy auto racing ten or fifteen years ago.

I've never seen such a wide variety of sponsors as there are in auto racing. In the future, the cars and drivers will have to be bigger so that there's enough room for all those sponsors' patches. Auto racing has an "accelerating" effect on the fans, but you know, and I know, most are there to see parts and sparks flying through the air after a crash. At the major races, half the people go there for the partying; the race is secondary.

I know there are gonna be some good old boys and some of my friends who won't agree with me on this. But frankly, I don't consider auto racing a sport. The result of a race depends more on machinery than a human being. I'm not taking anything away from the drivers' athletic ability. They have tremendous skills and strength and a huge pair of balls. But all those skills won't do you any good when you run out of gas on the last lap. Auto, motorcycle, motorboat, and even a horse, whatever you're sitting on, or in, runs out of fuel. It doesn't give the person much of a sporting chance to win.

All of you people who treat your cars better than most people do, don't get upset. It's just a bartender's opinion. I'm far from being a car enthusiast. To me, a car is no more than a means of transportation; as long as it gets me there, I'm happy.

The last three years I lived in Fort Myers Beach, I didn't own or need a car. And I loved it.

• Tennis is a sport I was always going to play; I just haven't gotten around to it yet. I've always enjoyed watching the sport and understand the strategy and the rules pretty well, for not ever playing the sport. I did play a lot of ping-pong in my life; I think that helps me enjoy watching it. It wasn't called table tennis in North Toledo.

Tennis, like golf, used to be a rich man's sport. But in the last fifty years, when middle-class America's income rose, it became more affordable, and therefore more people have the opportunity to play. When it became necessary to have two paychecks per family for maintaining a better lifestyle, and "charge it" became a part of our everyday vocabulary, low-mid America bought more adult toys and found more recreational outlets for relaxation. That's when tennis and golf became available and were played more by people other than the country club set.

Athleticism is only one of the things that is outstanding in tennis. The conditioning and endurance required are remarkable, and it is truly amazing how a player can make his mind tell his body to keep going after three and four hours in the hot sun. It's a testament to the mental and physical strength it takes for a person to compete in tennis. My mother used to say, "Don't ever marry a tennis player; to them love is nothing."

• When I moved to Florida in the middle eighties, I was still playing softball and a lot of golf, but after a year or two, they fell by the wayside. That's when I got into beach volleyball. With the sun, sand, cooler full of lemonade (Bud Light), and skimpy bathing suits with happy, healthy people to boot, I was in paradise.

The first time I watched the pros play in Fort Myers, when they started touring the country, I was hooked. To watch two people cover the court, run and jump in that hot sand for hours was a mind-blower; I'm talking about some fine-tuned, well-conditioned athletes. To this day, I think they're some of the best athletes in the world.

Volleyball's got all the athletic movement and skill spectators like: long-legged women in spandex shorts or bikinis help give it a big lift in popularity among men. But I'm afraid it won't ever get to be a major sport on TV, unless they wire the net with electricity.

• It marvels me how people can take pro wrestling seriously; it's like life today, where sensationalism rules. Take pro wrestling, the six o'clock news, and the pet rock; when they marketed them into believability, I saw how easily people will follow the crowd; it scared me.

When a 280-pound man can jump off the top rope onto another man and that man who was supposed to have had his Adam's apple crushed into applesauce gets up and kicks his ass, that's about as believable as one of our former leaders testifying in court and not being able to recall sixteen hundred times.

They're good athletes and their acrobatic skills are excellent. But wrestling's nothing but a gymnastic comedy stag play. It is a theatrical performance with muscular men, sexy women, and a few midgets, all beating each other over the head with metal chairs, and a blind referee who can't count to four! They should say, "Let's get ready to *laugh*," not "rumble."

You see athletes punching each other out in the stands, locker rooms, during interviews, everywhere but in the ring, and when they're in the ring, they do everything but wrestle; and the comedy is complete when you see women with all their sex parts hanging out punching men, acting like they're tough. Managers cheap-shot the opponents of their wrestlers. Promoters yell at each other and fight to hype up the ... I guess you would call them fans, and bury each other's face in the crack of some sweaty slog's ass. What fanfare, oooooh. If that's what sports is all about, no sportsmanship or rules, none that are enforced anyway, we're sending a message to our youth that character and credibility don't matter as long as you get rich.

If you are an adult, there's no problem if you want to watch this event. That's what freedom of choice is all about in America. But let's think about children who jump on each other's spine, knee each other in the stomach, and bloody each other's face. Teens are copying the marketed TV crap and filming themselves inflicting brutality and pain on one another, thinking it's cool. If you call this a sport, you must have something against children. Frankly speaking, pro wrestling is like watching the same movie over and over and over, where the ending is always the same.

Amateur collegiate style wrestling is the only form of wrestling that can be called a sport. These athletes show character and sportsmanship that should get big-time publicity. I think colleges should embrace sports principles that promote character and real sportsmanship, but the boards of directors of colleges are eliminating these programs. Evidently scholarships for education don't have the same importance as monetary gain. If a collegiate wrestler were able to use metal chairs and fake blood, and college girls in bikinis were allowed to mud wrestle, then the boards of directors would be happy to market these for profit, and I betcha that then they would find room for these in their athletic program budgets.

• I never liked to fight. But for some reason, I've been a boxing fan all my life. I guess I like to think of it as it used to be: two men doing the best they can to win, within the rules that govern true sportsmanship.

Boxing had good intentions about sportsmanship when it started. But it went from the Marquis of Queensbury rules to whoever has the agent with the best Mafia ties. Boxing and horse racing have been in Mafia control longer than any other sport I can think of. I mean, not just the Mafia that's sensationalized in movies, or the front man with the electric shock hair-do who gets all the publicity on TV, but the other kind, the ones behind the scenes that control the real money, the business Mafia.

I mentioned earlier being a bag man for a family in Toledo many a moon ago. I know a little more than most about the money bet on boxing. I also tended bar at the racetrack where the thoroughbreds used to run. There, I watched owners who didn't bet on their own horses, but the one they knew was going to win. I also heard, from my invisible place behind the bar, conversations of owners and gamblers about the fixing of races. My knowledge of this subject is not a punch in the dark. I've been around the track a few times.

Yes, it's brutal sometimes, but boxing is on the ropes. It doesn't have as much uncontrolled mayhem or sensationalism as ultimate fighting and pro wrestling have to market. It's hard to compete against fighting like that when you have to wear gloves and obey a referee who knows how to count to ten.

• Ultimate fighting sucks, unless you have a little psycho in you. I've seen enough fighting in bars and the streets to last me a lifetime. It's like living in today's world. People think it's cool to inflict as much pain as possible on someone, just to be Number One. Don't all you macho people get upset and loud. You don't have to take my ear off; it's just a view.

• The Olympic Dream Team is a good example of what our lust for profit and being Number One has escalated to. The thrill of the Olympics used to be watching amateur athletes doing their best to dig down deep inside to pull off the upset, against all odds. Win or lose, we took pride in the fact we weren't cheating like we thought the Russians were. And, for some amateur athletes, the Olympics were their springboard to the pros.

It wasn't fair the way Russia stacked their teams with men who played together all year round and were like pros. That would play against our younger men and boys who had only weeks to practice together as a team. But Russia did it for propaganda, not so much for money.

Our American Olympic committee threw amateurism and the principles of the Olympian idea out of the window when we sent our professionals to the Olympics, which was like sending Rembrandt to a finger painting contest. Our reason was not for propaganda, but for the money and attention gained in being Number One. That's when the money power of media hype pushed the idea that we have to let the pros play so that America can win. And the "follow the crowd" American fan jumps on the bandwagon, not caring about the tradition of amateurism.

In 1980, America's hockey team upset the Russians in the Olympics. That was far more exciting and a part of our great

Olympic memory, and will be remembered a lot longer than any Dream Team.

Frankly speaking, the Olympics is just one of many things in America showing that the sense of fair play doesn't have a sporting chance.

• I have been criticizing the TV industry for its handling of sports, but I will give it credit for helping women athletes have a better opportunity to get college scholarships and some of the professional sports, money that was long overdue. When women stopped worrying about "that's not ladylike" and gained the numbers to create teams and establish leagues, they were off and running.

Not many girls played sports when I was young. And if they did, they were called tomboys, which was a put-down. My older sister, Pat, played sports with my older brother, Gene, and me and other boys in the neighborhood, and competed as well as most, and better than some. She wasn't bad with her dukes, either. If anybody picked on me, they had to deal with Pat. Watching her compete in sports and play as well as most boys, I knew it was only a matter of time before more girls would forget about the criticism, and women in sports would be as accepted as men.

In the adult sports world, muscle eventually takes over. At pee-wee and in some cases junior level, girls playing sports on teams dominated by boys is fine. They wouldn't be there if they weren't good enough. When girls get into their teens, I don't believe they should compete in sports against boys for the simple reason of physics. What is there to prove that's worth the risk of being injured for life? It's bad enough that young men who are bigger and stronger get maimed or worse. If girls stay in a sport that's dominated by males, eventually the physical demand will be so great that a girl's best won't do. And their chances of getting to the upper echelon of that sport are slim to none. Co-ed sports, which I play and enjoy, with women and men on the same team, are no problem. But all-men physical sports are a different ballgame.

It's a no-brainer for women trying to compete against men in sports where physical strength outweighs skills. Women have overcome a lot of things, but unless male and female body design changes, who's physically stronger is a dead issue. Whoever drew up the blueprints saw to that. Besides, most men don't want to arm-wrestle with women. Though when I quarterbacked in football, I always thought a female center would have been cool.

As I look back, I think my sister got away with playing sports with guys only because times were different then. Young men had more chivalry and were taught that hitting a girl wasn't a manly thing to do. But those days are gone.

Women are great athletes. Their competitiveness, intensity and skills should have been enough to make women in sports a marketing item. But ever since censorship lost out to marketing, the exploitation of sex has brought women's sports from obscurity to prime time.

The spandex that highlights every nook and cranny, the sheer bra for the sweaty-nipple look, and cameras with zoom lenses to give you a close-up of the nooks and crannies have made the sex fan tune in. No one's going to tell me these aren't done for marketing sex. (Marketing sex in sports is best "illustrated" in the swimsuit issue of the top-selling sports magazine.)

At one summer Olympics, the American women's soccer team got more publicity from a girl taking her shirt off than from the fact that they won. A lot of the draw that helped wrestling get a hold on the ratings is a woman's sweaty, jiggling body covered only by a handful of cloth. As for women's boxing, men have always gotten off on women fighting. Now they can have it right in their own front room. If you check out the audience, there aren't enough women in the stands to pay the light bill.

Frankly speaking, if there's one thing a man doesn't have a sporting chance in against women, it is the overtime periods in the game of sex.

• My older brother, Gene, beat me in every sport we played when we were young. He didn't believe in letting me win. I used to get pissed off, but it taught me about losing and made me a very aggressive competitor. Every sport I played with the aggressiveness that I had to use against my brother, just to have a chance to win. Frankly speaking, I wasn't the best in any one sport I played, but above average in all (it carried over to my other endeavors in life).

Some say I was a bad sport when I lost; now that I'm older, I'll admit it, I was at times. But to this day, you show me someone who likes to lose and I'll show you a loser. I still don't like to lose. But after too many golf clubs broken in getting mad at myself and mentally beating myself up too many times after a bad round, I've mellowed out. A guy named Zeto helped me out.

When I played softball, I was a hothead and got carried away once in a while. Around 1975, when working in a bar, I helped the owner hire bands. The lead singer of one band I hired was also a good softball player. I got him on our softball team. He was about nine years younger than I, and his Tasmanian devil nature on the ball field made me look like an amateur at getting mad about losing. Watching him blow got me to look at myself.

Zeto turned out to be one of my best friends; his name is Larry, but to people who knew him well, it's Zeto (you had to have a nickname if you were a good athlete growing up in North Toledo).

Zeto was a Dr. Jekyll and Mr. Hyde. On the field of play, to put it mildly, he was unlikable. But when he wasn't competing in sports, he was one of the nicest guys you could ever know. People who never saw him in a game when Hyde came out couldn't believe the stories about his antics, and the people who knew him from sports couldn't believe he was a nice person and a good singer when they saw Dr. Jekyll on stage.

Zeto and I and a couple other buddies were roommates back in the seventies. He had an Afro hairdo that was a foot and a half wide, and I shaved my head shiny bald. When we played ball together, or when he was singing in the bar and I was bartending, we looked like a before-and-after hair transplant commercial.

• When I coached grade-school football, I watched young boys turn into men. Some boys who played for me in my first few years came back ten or so years later and helped me coach. At one time, they had aspirations of becoming pros. Most of them never got to college, but those who did ended up back in the hood with a useless piece of paper to hang on the wall, or in one case, a cardboard box home.

With this personal experience tucked away in my head, living on the beach years after my coaching days were over, I thought a lot about young men in this situation. It is perfectly fine for young men to spend four years playing football in college (in reality, it's the farm system for the NFL). Even if they don't make the pros, they receive four years of paid schooling. College sports is a business, more than a learning program. Sports scholarships are granted for the sole purpose of making money for the college. Education is not the main factor in their decision to hand out these scholarships. They just want athletes to play a sport that will fill the stands on Saturdays and make the school money from TV contracts. A young man's future doesn't enter the minds of the administrators. If he wants to play college football, and have a chance to make the pros and make money, let's be honest about it: It's hard work to get through college. My son had to put in a lot of time and hard work to get his degree.

The biggest share of college athletes comes from a lower-class background, and some have had a difficult time getting through high school. They can't even carry the books for college courses without the help of the college administrators padding their programs with weak, made-for-athletes courses. Athletes spend a third of their time going to two-a-day practices, an hour watching films, and traveling a day or two each week as well as going to lengthy team meetings. Unless they were faking or holding back in high school, how the hell can they pass college courses? All this makes a college degree look cheap.

Going to college without getting a real education is not an advantage to the athlete or the full-time student. For the athletes who don't make the pros, they still can receive four years of education, as long as they keep their grades up. When they're a little older, with the illusion of a sports career behind them, they see things from a different perspective, and want to better themselves. They realize the value of an education and how important it is to have a profession rather than going back to the same background with a useless degree, wholly dejected with a bad attitude. They can go back with credentials under their belt, and do something constructive for their community, something to improve the standard of living in their area and become *real* role models.

Then you wouldn't have the full-time student seeing the college handing out freebie degrees to athletes, when he himself had to work hard and make sacrifices to earn his degree. Also, we wouldn't be preprogramming young adults into thinking that cheating or corruption is the way our system functions and that being honest and truthful is a joke.

I know this idea wouldn't work for everyone; some athletes would go to the pros early, and some, after four years of playing sports, wouldn't want the education they had worked for. Frankly speaking, I believe the overall result would be for the better.

• I've played, coached, and followed football most of my life. It used to be the rule of thumb that blacks couldn't play quarterback (definitely a white racist, control assumption). When successful black quarterbacks couldn't be ignored anymore and started to get drafted by the pros, they were subject to ridicule by racists, and their mistakes were magnified out of proportion, making it harder for them to prove themselves. They might make the same mistakes a white quarterback would make, but theirs wouldn't be passed off as human error; you constantly heard critics say, "Blacks aren't as smart as whites." (When you're afraid of making a mistake, you're very likely going to make one.)

In the late sixties, early seventies, when the black quarterback vs. white quarterback controversy became the subject for the armchair quarterback (bar dweller), I didn't get into the debate too much. I felt there was something else to it. I knew too many young black players I had coached who were too intelligent and competent to be classified as "dumb by color." Years after coaching, while sitting on Fort Myers Beach, where

I could get into deep, uninterrupted thought, I came up with a view about the black quarterback subject, based on my own coaching experiences. Since then, I've talked to black friends and to strangers about my view, and I have to say it hasn't been discredited.

I coached black and white quarterbacks of average intelligence, who were not that good academically. After two or three years with me, they knew all the plays, and counter-plays, to use when things broke down. When the play would break down, they would hang in there and be able to make a snap decision naturally, reacting as they had been coached. I had black quarterbacks who had excellent grades in school and above-average intelligence. Being with me two or three years made them know the plays as well as I did. But there were occasions when instead of making the snap decision I knew they were capable of, they would panic and start running. At practice, I would ask them why, and usually I got a shrug of the shoulders or a blank look.

Just a view: Blacks, after generations of preprogramming and not being able to make decisions freely, are being punished, ridiculed, and told "You're wrong," even when they're right, by white authority. I believe this historical experience has something to do with the way my players reacted, and maybe why I got the shrugged-shoulders response. Possibly locked away in their heads was the fear of making a wrong decision, being thought of as a dumb black; and that put their brain on hold for that instant, when it was supposed to react.

Coaching back in the sixties and early seventies when the Civil Rights movement was gaining momentum, I noticed that black subservient mindset was still prevalent in most households. Then I watched a change. Black parents and leaders started teaching their children the value of being yourself, to be proud of who you are and not let the color of your skin hold you back. Now black quarterbacks with more freedom of thought, being psychologically stronger, know such mistakes are human error, and not because "I'm a dumb black."

Blacks' natural athletic ability has been misunderstood and criticized by white sports fans as long as I can remember. The false conception about their athletic skills comes from early white Christianity teaching that blacks evolved from primates. It's simply a fact that their physical makeup and muscle structure was adapted for survival in their environment.

• Frankly speaking, sports have allowed opportunities for many low-income youngsters to get a better education than they would have been able to receive otherwise. It's a shame, though, that many low-income youngsters' potential is not met because they lack athletic ability, and don't win scholarships. My view has a few bumps to smooth out, but it's better than what we're dealing with now.

• The officiating in sports today reflects the double standards prevalent in America's inconsistency in who's right or who's wrong. Referees either have Alzheimer's, or don't remember that the foul they called earlier has happened again, but this time, it's not called.

The official's pre-game warm-up consists of a list of players who are marketing starts and who get special treatment. Like announcers, they give good calls to the good guy who's marketed as a role model, and bad calls to the marketed bad guy. They know when and when not to blow the whistle to make sure the series goes seven games for TV marketing, and to get more money in their own pockets.

Getting the home team the right calls has always been part of the game. But now, in which arena the game is played makes no difference; what makes the difference is that players are the ones who are the big marketing item. Frankly speaking, they should change the word "officiating" to "judgment calling."

• I wish athletes today would quit taking runs at their opponents when they're not looking, with unsportsmanlike cheap shots. No one's going to feel worse than they when they get older and realize they put a young man in a wheelchair for the rest of his life, or even killed him. It will hit them someday that it wasn't that important. And, don't athletes on TV know we can read lips?

• A long time ago, a bar owner friend of mine said I should "quit playing sports so much and use that energy to make money." What I finally realized, years later, was that money may be needed for survival, but I couldn't have survived without sports. I can't remember not being sports-minded. I'm sure my older brother, Gene, had a lot to do with it. We made a sporting event out of anything we could create competition in. Frankly speaking, there wouldn't have been this book, *Frankly Speaking*, without my love of sports. I wouldn't have been able to escape from dwelling on the negative side in my younger years if it weren't for my imagination transporting me to my "field of dreams." Whether I was in Toledo, Florida, or Texas, my ability on the field of play helped me fit in.

Sports instilled confidence, competitiveness, and a desire to excel, at whatever, without being afraid of a new challenge, as well as other pluses that have been beneficial in later years. The paranoia and insecurity that might have been were replaced by physical and mental health and strength. Sports also had an educational value for me. "H-O-R-S-E" was one of the first words that I was sure I spelled correctly.

To this day, the outside world gets put on "pause" when I'm competing in sports. It's my justification for thinking, "There are a lot of things I've done, but a lot more I haven't tried yet." I'll be real frank with you: Playing sports is my drug, and I still have the need for a fix.

Chapter X

MEDIA

If "the pen is mightier than the sword," why does the sword get all the headlines? If I ever write a book exclusively about the media, it would be about how the media have preprogrammed Americans to be a herd of misinformed, misled readers and viewers who believe what they're getting is the truth.

I grew up in a newspaper-minded family. I don't remember my age when I used to lie on the floor with my brother and sisters, trading sections of the paper to read. Listening to the news on the radio was a family tradition, and we never missed my mother's favorite, Walter Winchell. This carried through to the TV newscast in 1949 when we got our first TV

I didn't realize until years later, after reading books about history and current events, that what I grew up reading in school history books and seeing in the news was only the partial truth, sometimes an outright lie.

As a bartender, I found out a long time ago that more than 75 percent of the people I talked to or observed got most of their knowledge about politics, world and current events, including sports, movies, history, health, etc., from TV, newspapers, and news magazines. And if I, or anyone else, would elaborate beyond information available from TV, newspapers, and magazines, others usually would cop an attitude or call you a liar.

And when it was one of the bar's favorite topics, the presidency, some people usually ended up in an argument or a fight. No matter how bad the news about the person they had voted for, people wouldn't accept the fact that they voted for a loser. It's funny how most people are afraid to admit being wrong. Frankly speaking, I wonder, why people want to believe that one man can run a corporation the size of America?

Even with the media's double-standard way of reporting half truths (decades too late and one-sided most of the time), we're getting more news and information about corruption of government, politics, and politicians and the hidden secrets and dark side of religions, the real reasons for war, assassination of political and world leaders, the false and phony side of mega Hollywood and sport stars, company and stock fraud, and scandals of anyone they catch with their pants down. But no one will expose the financial control of the world banks or international bankers, which are Siamese twins. And if you try, you won't get to first base in the mainstream media, simply because all major news agencies are puppets controlled by the Puppeteers (bankers who control their purse strings).

For decades, the three major TV networks had a lock on what information in the news could be reported. Editors and high-ranking staff members were trained not to let information that could hurt the Puppeteers or anyone on their money team get to the people, until the word arrangers could make it either misleading or confusing, and if that wasn't possible, they simply swept it under the rug. All that has changed with the emergence of computers, cable, and satellite TV. More numerous outlets have made the control of information almost impossible.

The competition to be first to report a story is a priority for top rating and the marketing power that comes with it. If you don't report a story on one of the insiders, the new kids on the block will, since being first means money. Information on wrongdoing isn't to be stifled like in the past. Years ago, the pecker tracks on the blue dress wouldn't have been reported by the mainstream press until the man was long gone from office.

The media double standards of reporting are a prime example of how our preprogrammed society functions. The word arrangers can have you think an accident is a tragedy or a tragedy an accident. Who's wrong when they're right? Who's not guilty when they're guilty?

When the press is sticking the camera in the face of people, badgering them with questions; hanging out to dry someone who can't defend himself because of status or situation; attacking someone who, at one time, was protected by the system but screwed up too many times and became vulnerable, media, to make it sound like they're just doing their job, will use the phrase, "The people have the right to know." The people have the right to know the *truth* is the way it should be said.

If the truth were known by the public about the media's behind-closed-doors involvement in world affairs, control of political puppets, and disinformation tools for the government, right down to the price of corn, then the people wouldn't be so easily duped into being got-to-have-it consumers, voting for corrupt politicians, accepting perjury by a president, or becoming soldiers (pawns) who die in wars the Puppeteers create for greed and power.

The media's double standards of hand picking the people to expose or defend are determined by which money power is in control of the news source. One major news service will present a view of guilt and another of innocence. This confusion results only when you're someone in a prominent position and close to the Puppeteers. But, if you're a nobody who can't retaliate, they'll hit you on both sides, with no mercy.

One example of this came from sports a few years back, when, as I mentioned earlier, the superstar role model spit in an umpire's face. Because of his marketing value for TV playoff money to be made, he got a slap on the hand and it was never made an issue by the media.

Another ballplayer, at about the same time, made a remark about the New York ethnic populace with a few true statements that the press turned into racial slurs. This man didn't say anything more than stand-up comedians say in comedy clubs all across America, where everybody roars with laughter at how funny it is. But because this athlete is a controversial character, and outspoken, when he mentioned the word "Jew," the New York press's hunger for sensationalism made him look like a racist villain. Not only did they blow the incident out of proportion, but they also tried to ruin his career for speaking his mind. They dogged him so bad he got suspended and fined for exercising his freedom of speech. The press made it look like he was off his rocker. In reality, all he did is mention the word "Jew" in the wrong city—New York.

• The media are right on top of reporting riots; in fact, they often get there before the police do. The brutal beating by the L.A. police a few years ago of Rodney "why don't we all get along, guys" King is an example of five or six policemen beating him as if he had just molested their mothers. The media, to keep the hate juices going, made sure the beating was shown every twenty minutes or so on TV.

Anybody who saw the tape knows that was excessive use of force by the police. It was somewhere between being in a frenzy and having fun. When the word arrangers got the jury to believe that all the well-armed police were scared and in fear of their lives, they were pronounced Not Guilty.

At the time, I was with a girlfriend and her daughter in Florida, returning from a trip to Disney World. When the verdict came over the radio, I told her, "There will be rioting in L.A. tonight." If millions of Americans other than myself who heard that not-guilty verdict knew what was going to happen, how come the L.A. authorities didn't? The media knew, and got there before it started.

If you have read as much as I have about all the taxpayers' money that local government officials receive to rebuild after riots and how much of it goes into their pockets, not to mention kickbacks from contractors and developers, it might explain why they don't react until such situations are already out of control. This is when the media and the government team up, for financial reasons. The media make money by marketing the stories they cram down our throats, and the taxpayers' money to rebuild keeps the bureaucrats fat and happy.

On the tube, you can see looters carrying armloads of merchandise from stores, while the National Guard and police, with orders not to interfere, stand there and watch. Two days later, the politicians blamed the police for not protecting the businesses and pampering the looters, saying, "They're just victims of circumstance, reacting to the situation."

Has no one on the L.A. authority staff ever heard of preventive measures, or did they simply look the other way, being slow to react, knowing it would be a big payday for everyone on the home team? For the media, it's the usual double-standard reporting, blaming everybody but the right ones, and making lots of money marketing the stories.

• When was the last time a personality contest didn't determine the outcome of a presidential election? Not since the news industry turned the American public into visual news robots. Platforms or issues take a back seat to the importance of being a good orator, with charisma, and better than average in appearance. It makes no difference who's better qualified or has more experience for the position. If they don't possess a good TV marketing image, they don't have a chance.

The first time the significance of the TV image was seen as a necessity for the presidency was when Stevenson ran against Eisenhower in the fifties. Stevenson was the person better qualified, but his old-fashioned pride and sense of honor wouldn't allow him to lower himself for TV promotional ads. Ike's backers used the TV ads to their advantage, and the rest is history.

The head of CBS, Mr. Paley, was sitting with Goldwater when Reagan read a Nixon acceptance speech at the Republican Convention in '68. He said to Goldwater, "We're going to make him president," because of his professionalism in front of the camera, not his political ability. The financial powers started the plan to market him for the presidency.

Political financial backers (soft money) and election committees realized that the TV image was the main factor in presidential elections when Kennedy, who was a charismatic orator, but not as experienced as Nixon, won the election with his personality and good looks, presenting a more positive and winning image than the straight-faced, nervous Nixon in TV debates. Frankly speaking, if Kennedy, with his stronger TV image in the debates, had not upset the Berkley Mafia's protégé, Nixon, he just possibly might still be alive today.

Since Kennedy, only a few presidents have been in office without the TV image being the main factor. Johnson won in '64 mainly because people associated him with the Kennedy administration and his inside political power. Ford got in because he was doing what he was told, as the prosecutor for the Warren commission. When the Republicans ran Dole against Clinton in '96, I knew they didn't want to win, or they knew they couldn't. If they had wanted to win, they sure would have come up with a better TV image than Dole presented.

• The press will do whatever it takes to protect the president in office because there are too many paparazzi on the loose to keep lies hidden for long. The tactic used now by the media is to confuse and mislead the people with its double-standard technique of word arranging.

Willie Boy was not the first or the last president who received preferential treatment by the media while he was in office. It was a genuine snow job the media whipped on the people during Willie Boy's sex scandal and impeachment cases. If you turned on one of the major news channels, it might be pro-Starr, presenting Willie Boy in a bad light. Turn to another news network, they downplay the sexual harassment and make it sound like just a little sex thing, no big deal. Another station might blame the political opposition for picking on him. People were making decisions about right or wrong according to their favorite news show.

He's not the only president to get a head job in the Oral Office. With the help of the media, Willie Boy got away with perjury. The press sugar-coated his not answering questions, his "I don't recall" sixteen hundred times, and "What is 'is'?"

Privileged people are protected by the aristocratic doctrine of double standards employed by the media. In one court, Willie Boy can get away with perjury, while in another, a judge might sentence Mr. or Mrs. Everyday Citizen five years for perjury, even though all they did was lie to protect a loved one on a minor felony like possession of an ounce of marijuana.

In my opinion, there are controversial issues about the Clintons that many people still wonder about. Eventually I believe he'll be blamed for the downturn in the economy. And when the media cut loose on his wife, they will really keep the people glued to the tube. When he was in office, the leader of our country spent a million dollars a year for defense attorneys. I believe that whenever he does have to stand up to face the music, it will all be forgotten and covered up. All he'll receive is a slap on the hand and plenty of media hoopla.

The only good thing that will come out of this is that maybe people in the future will see the importance of knowing before voting who the president really works for. For you to obtain a job, would you spend millions to make a few hundred thousand in return? The media and entertainment industry make celebrities of serial killers and other murderers who have the gore and horrendous sensationalism in their crimes that can be easily marketed.

• Our legal system will keep a serial killer alive for years, during which time the killer will get the celebrity notoriety and the attention he or she was seeking. Money made from books and movie rights that the legal profession secures for these lowlifes (and takes a cut of) will keep them alive with all the appeals money can buy. Also, the killer becomes a marketing item for the media and movie industry, where profit is more important than right or wrong.

The victim's loved ones are used by the media right after the crime, when they play up the grief angle to get public sympathy, but are soon forgotten and replaced by new grieving loved ones. The victim's loved ones have to suffer heartbreak and mental anguish plus financial strain for years, with no media or anyone else giving a damn about their situation.

The killer gets dragged around the country, showing where and how the crime was committed ten years ago, and the whole time Mr. and Mrs. Citizen pick up the tab for the money spent on public officials and transportation, along with the three squares a day for this person who should be dead or put away and forgotten. And if that isn't enough, the blood-lust media will play it up big time, with their double-standards excuse, "The people have the right to know," without concern about opening old wounds of the victim's loved ones.

• When I was tending bar in the early seventies, I'd already had at least ten years of watching and reading how the press was misleading the American public. In discussions with people my age and older about current affairs of the day and the recent past, I realized something about the American people. One of the hardest things to do is to get Americans to believe the truth if it's different from the one-sided view the media presented, and I'm afraid that still holds true today.

When I used to tell people that there was no way Oswald could have been the only gunman that day in Dallas, and that he might not have been the one at all, most people thought I was out to lunch. When I told people that Pearl Harbor happened because England was going under and we had to bail them out, and the money was already being spent for war preparations, most people didn't believe me or wanted to fight. Working in a factory in '71, I was talking to my buddies at work about Vietnam, telling them it was nothing but war games for the Pentagon, Nixon was lying through his teeth, and young boys were dying for nothing. Possibly the Kennedy assassination was linked to his wanting to pull out of Vietnam. At that time, my son was about seven years old. I told my buddies I would never let my son die for this government (I never said America). Well, my buddies called me a communist and wanted to tar and feather me. But in less than ten years, most of those who argued with me thanked me for letting them see another view closer to the truth.

The press lied right along with our government leaders on the Iraq (Desert Storm) fiasco. While "read my lips" George was saying "We will not go to war," behind the scenes the money was already being spent for war. The first couple of days after the first invasion of Iraq, the mainstream news channels had twenty-four-hour coverage. Because of their need to keep the American public glued to the tube, they had to create stories to fill the gaps in the war games (the reason I watch the news is to see the latest lies the media are selling).

There was more, but I especially remember two stories that speak for themselves. One was about the troops brought in from Europe. While they were getting off a transport plane, a woman reporter was interviewing a high-ranking officer. As they were marching by the camera with heavy green khaki uniforms on, the reporter asked the officer why they didn't have on the light-colored Desert Storm camouflage uniforms. Without thinking, the officer said, "They should have. We had ordered them *months ago*, but they haven't arrived yet."

The second story: The media were reporting stories about the war effort at home. They did a story on one of the Goodwill factories that was making Desert Storm products. When interviewing the head administrator, the reporter was praising the job the handicapped workers were doing, and the administrator said, "We've been working on these for months," even though this was just days after "read my lips" George was on the tube telling the American people, "We have no intention of going to war."

From our satellite surveillance to intelligence information, we knew Iraq was building troops up there on the border of Kuwait. I think the sensible thing would have been for the U.N. to stop them before the invasion, not wait until the damage was done. After the invasion, the press, to justify the Pentagon's spending our tax dollars, tells the American public, "We had to come to their rescue and protect their human rights from this madman Hussein." Remember the old adage: "People who live in glass houses shouldn't throw stones." The media and government should put as much effort and expense into the human rights issues right here at home as they do running around the world spending money on wars while using human rights as an excuse.

With the second war with Iraq and the second Bush, after the young lives lost and all the money wasted, the same madman we left in power would be used again. But this time, the excuse used for wasting human lives and money is terrorism and weapons of mass destruction.

• When the media does print the truth about wars, it is always a decade or more too late and not of much use to the everyday people whose money was already wasted and lives lost. When I was young, I hated the Nazis and Japs. The older I got, I started feeling sorry for them, as I do for all people dying all over the world today for no reason at all, except for preprogrammed hate.

• For the last sixty years, the reason for every war that the media sold the American public was a fabricated lie. And the results are always the same—young men and innocent people die so that the people who create wars and escalate them make money. The Puppeteers have their puppets that dangle at the ends of the purse strings.

I've read and heard it said by our military strategists, "War is a chess game." They're absolutely right. The pawns are sacrificed to protect the king.

The American taxpayers fall into the media trap, whenever the latter use human rights, patriotism, communism, or, now, terrorism. The media cleverly and successfully present their version of why there was no alternative to war. Being convinced of falsehoods, people pay no attention to how the money is being wasted by the war industry and how many young men and women are sacrificed.

We have soldiers all over the world protecting American conglomerates that buy the country's government officials, so their companies can take advantage of cheap labor and lack of environmental laws, and pay no taxes or other expenses they would have to pay in America. They ship their cheaply made goods back to America to sell at one hell of a profit. If it weren't for oil companies owned by the Puppeteers, we wouldn't have had this big military buildup in the Middle East for the last half of a century. The biggest share of the countries the press calls "anti-American" are just pissed off at what damage America's money is responsible for, not Americans.

• Where do the people in Third World countries, wearing our old Goodwill hand-me-downs and sandals, who can't afford to eat or live in a decent dwelling, get the thousands of dollars worth of armaments hanging on their bodies? If the media's so-called in-depth reporting weren't so shallow, they would expose our government and other world governments that pass out weapons like candy, right after the Puppeteers get people mad enough to use them by loudly and constantly proclaiming and propagating through double-standard words that fit the occasion, such as "human rights," "patriotism," "communism," "terrorism," and the biggie, "religion." Our military doesn't care about the unnecessary loss of life; to them, this "collateral damage" is just job security, pure and simple. The Pentagon doesn't pay for them; we taxpayers do through the Pentagon. Don't forget that America has long been the biggest weapons-dealer in the world.

• Because of the freedom to say what I've felt through my life, I've been told quite a few times, and probably will hear it again, "If you don't like America, leave it," or sometimes more bluntly, "Get out." That I love America so much is what gives me the motivation for speaking my mind. And that's why I hope to get people constantly talking about freedom to express their own views and enjoy their freedom of speech. Tending bar, frankly speaking, I've sometimes been told by people, "Be careful, you shouldn't be talking like that." I guess I've never been afraid of Big Brother's hearing me. I don't preach revolution or violence. I just try to get people to look and hear with an open mind, not with the preprogrammed mind that simply makes people blindly follow the crowd. Frankly speaking, that's what our American freedom is all about.

• The Puppeteers who've controlled media have misinformed us on historical facts about World War II to keep the hate juices flowing in one direction. The Japanese got a slap on the hand, compared to bad press the Germans got on the crimes they committed against their captives. The Japanese got bombed with atomic weapons, but they had bombed us first; the Germans didn't.

Not until the last decade or so have the media and its TV affiliates like the History Channel and public television channels revealed the inhumane medical experiments the Japanese performed on the Chinese people. But as long as I can remember, from high school history, movies, magazines, and TV programs that were supposed to have special historical significance, there were only stories about Germans using Jews for medical experiments; not the Japanese atrocities, nor those of the American government conducting experiments on blacks without their knowledge or permission.

Japan attacked America; Germany didn't. For years, the media have given the Japanese a more favorable image than the Germans. At anniversaries of World War II battles in the Pacific, you will see American and Japanese soldiers arm-in-arm with no animosity toward each other, reminiscing about their experiences. How many times have you seen the same scenario with American and German soldiers? The only portrayal of Germans by the media industry was of Hitler, the goose step and piles of dead bodies. Historians have called Pearl Harbor a tragedy, but it was no accident that we were not informed about the coming attack until it was too late.

The History Channel and public TV are controlled by the same money that owns the other media industry, with 80 percent of writers, directors, and producers being Jewish. This could have something to do with Hitler's being on TV for the last fifty years, more than any other historical figure. Frankly speaking, the press is slick about the way they make news from the news they previously kept away from the public.

• The media are pros at presenting lurid war scenes. It's all about points on the TV rating scale, not about the truth. The press showed no respect for the feelings of families and their loved ones, the soldiers, being dragged through the streets of Mogadishu, Somalia. And when they were challenged about their low-life sensationalism, they defended themselves with the old stand-by, "The people have the right to know." And like magic, it went away and was all forgotten. I think the loved ones of all present and future soldiers should have "the right to know": Why have so many soldiers been killed trying to capture a few terrorists? The military made sure the terrorists got out first while American soldiers were left behind to die. And I wouldn't be afraid to bet that the terrorists were eventually released and the military, with the help of the press, will justify this disregard for American soldiers and scores of innocent people's lives by saying, "Oops, it's just the casualties of war." (The media will make it go away, to cover another day.)

For the first couple of weeks it was too obvious. That's the view the Puppeteers' controlled media presented to American viewers of the attack on America. We heard the Jewish news analysts, reporters, professionals, and celebrities spewing a lopsided barrage of hatred toward Muslims. Jumping on the bandwagon were senators, congressional representatives, and military people who got under-the-table money from conglomerates who manufacture weapons and war products. It was all about going to war and killing Muslims.

This is not about a race being blamed for anything. I would express this same view, with the same facts on this subject, if it were Irish, German, Polish, English, Chinese, or any other nationality. There's good and bad in all walks of life. I don't think the majority of any nationality should be blamed for a very small minority of greedy individuals.

I would like to put to rest any notion of my being anti-Semitic. I grew up in a Jewish neighborhood, with a synagogue on the corner of my block. We had one of the first TVs on our block. And every week, my mother invited three or four Jewish neighbors to watch *The Goldbergs*, a TV sitcom in the early fifties. I still have Jewish friends from the neighborhood whom I see from time to time, for example, Gary, who lived next door to me, and my buddy Poochie, who was my Friday night drinking partner in my early days. Poochie was a good athlete with whom I played sports into my adult years. I worked in a drug store for three years in my early teens for a Jew who was one of the kindest, fairest men I have ever known in my life. I don't hate Jews, or any other people. This is simply the way I think about this attack on America.

I want as much as anyone does to see the people responsible for 9/11 caught and prosecuted. In fact, they should be hanged by their nuts. But I'm glad we didn't go off half-cocked and bomb and kill a bunch of uneducated, misled, innocent people as we did in the past.

We know who crashed the planes into the buildings and blew themselves up. But for once in history, I would like to see those who planned it, ordered it, and profited from it be held responsible. Frankly speaking, this is my bartender's opinion. The banking families of the world, whom I call the Puppeteers, will be exposed someday. And when they are, you will find out they're behind all this chaos in the Middle East, using religion, with their controlled-media word arrangers keeping hate and violence in the headlines, while the real motive is the profit to be made from oil, 75 percent of the oil fields being in Muslim-controlled lands.

This attack on America goes back to what I mentioned earlier. As a bartender, I noticed that 80 percent of the people obtained their knowledge of important subjects from the media, and just as they did on Vietnam and other situations, the media always present a one-sided view.

• At noon on 9/11/2001, I was in a blue-collar bar called The Longhorn, in West Toledo. On 11/22/63, at noon, I was in a North Toledo blue-collar bar and people were glued to the TV. The looks on their faces were identical: the "deer in the headlights" look. This can't be happening in America. I also had that look in '63, and I believed the media's version then. But on 9/11, I knew there was more to this than meets the eye.

In '63, the attitude of the American people was different from what it is today. People were mad, but the violent mindset wasn't preprogrammed in everyone's head by the TV marketing industry like today.

The media didn't waste any time creating a hate atmosphere. In 2001, people didn't have time to dwell on remorse. Four hours after the first plane hit, before people had time to experience feelings for the dead and their loved ones, the media were showing people in Palestine burning the American flag and celebrating. These people saw this as a blow to our American government's backing of Israel and our sending weapons to kill Palestinians; there was no hatred for Americans as a whole. Our insensitive media put thousands of second- and third-generation American Muslims in harm's way, with prejudice and lopsided reporting, in the same way they tried to stir up the hate juices by falsely accusing Arabs within hours of the Oklahoma bombing, just because an Arab-looking person was in the area.

• When living in Florida during the war games called Desert Storm, I was outside at a beach tiki bar watching TV. Sitting and standing around the bar, watching this waste of life and resources, were tourists from the Midwest to the east coast and all the way South, executives, retirees, and people who worked and lived on the beach, an assortment of religions and nationalities, from six-figure incomes to five-dollars-an-hour people, all staring at the TV, letting the media whip them into a frenzy, and all yelling at the TV, "Kill the towel heads."

We were wrong in the past, letting the media preprogram people into thinking all Germans were Nazis, all Japanese were nips, all Vietnamese were gooks, and so on. Don't let the media make you believe all Muslims are terrorists. I don't remember the World Trade Towers having been a symbol of America in '93, when the same group tried to blow them up. But now, to create a war mindset among Americans, the media made the towers become a symbol. If they had blown up the Empire State Building, the Statue of Liberty, Boulder Dam, the Golden Gate Bridge, which *are* American icons, then I would feel more like it was an attack on America, but the WTC building is a symbol of financial wealth and worldwide economic control.

Acts of terrorism in America were inevitable and quite a few years ago al-Qaeda sent warnings. An act of terrorism in America is what they needed for the worldwide publicity they were seeking for their cause.

I've been reading for years how al-Qaeda was planning acts of terrorism in America. If the U.S. didn't quit sending to Israel arms that are used to kill and push Palestinians off the land they've been living on for ages, al-Qaeda warned us long before 9/11, there would be suicide bombers and hundreds of agents with vials of anthrax and cholera that were already in America. Two weeks before 9/11, Bin Laden was quoted in a London-published Muslim newspaper that there's something big coming down in America very soon. How come our high-ranking government officials didn't tighten up security on the suspected terrorists we knew were here? Why didn't the American media print information their top brass knew, which was being printed elsewhere around the world?

Our government had to know about the terrorists here in America, or else they did a good job of guessing their where-abouts. By 9/12, they were raiding apartments and homes of suspects, gathering information on terrorists that normally takes months, even years of investigating. I've never seen such a quick round-up of suspects and information about their locations and recent movements.

My bartending experience taught me not to judge who's right or wrong when listening to a one-sided version of a divorce. I knew I would be unable to make a fair assessment until I heard all sides of the story. I'm not justifying the suicide bombers and their accomplices; I think they're dead wrong. But why do their puppet leaders, who always make sure they're not the ones getting blown up, who brainwash these people into their religious fanaticism, always get away scot-free?

Suicide bombings are wrong. But it is equally wrong to shoot rockets into refugee camps and kill innocent people (who were booted out of their homes and mostly want no more than to survive). Such shooting and killing shouldn't be passed off by the media and American leaders as part of the war on terrorism, or as poor Israel's defense against terrorism.

This is just another form of guerrilla warfare. People throughout history, when fighting for a cause, have had to use whatever means possible when going up against military might. Israel has tanks and planes and plenty of other weapons, including nuclear weapons, while Palestinians have walking C-4 bombs and a religious cause.

I don't think American people would be too happy if the American Indians, with the help of some country with the military and financial power to back them, kicked Americans out of their homes and off their land and moved them into refugee camps and abused them, and then justified their actions by saying they lived there for far longer than a thousand years. I believe the Palestinians have lived in Israel for thousands of years, with unbroken continuity.

If it were a war and you attack a country, you wouldn't wait until a year later to strike back. The media word-arrangers tried their best to make the WTC suicide bombing look like it was an all-out attack on America. One of the first stories contrived was that Air Force One was a target. At the time, Howdy Doody was on the ground at a teacher conference in

Florida. Then they tried to sell the story that the White House was a target, to get the people scared and make them full of hatred. As for myself, I think the plane that crashed in Pennsylvania was also headed for the Pentagon, thus making two for the WTC building, and two for the Pentagon.

Their so-called madmen, who, by the way, were very well educated, knew it wouldn't do any good to kill Howdy Doody, because the Puppeteers would just replace him with another puppet. I would hate to think what would have happened if our ex-CIA vice-president might have gotten into the driver's seat. He would certainly have us in an all-out war in a heartbeat, by bombing half the Middle East, killing thousands of innocent people, and having more thousands of American soldiers sent home in body bags. He would have used Hussein again as an excuse to go to war. Then we would have an attack on America, which would turn loose hundreds of terrorists in America, resulting in millions of U.S. citizens ending up dead.

For fifty years, our government has sold to Americans the idea that we have the best air defense system in the world. We can have our planes in the air in a matter of minutes to knock down missiles, in most cases before they get to America. Why then, forty minutes after the first plane hit, did a plane hit our military nerve center, the Pentagon? The FAA knew before the first plane crashed that it was a terrorist attack and alerted our government officials. Where was our number-one air defense system that we, the taxpayers, have been paying for all these years? Frankly speaking, the reason no one got orders to do anything is that the Puppeteers wanted this to escalate into a war.

How many top military personnel were killed when that plane hit the Pentagon? I'm sure it didn't take them long to scurry to safety into their underground bunkers after they heard about the first plane hitting.

The 9/11 disasters were dirty, cowardly acts and I have nothing but contempt for the people responsible. But if I were the president, I would tell Israel that we will not abandon them and will do whatever it takes to protect them, but until we get this sorted out, we will cease sending military aid to Israel. The reason for this position is that I wish to make sure terrorists can't use our military support for Israel as an excuse to kill more American citizens.

• The men who planned and executed this taking of lives were not madmen as the media portrayed them to be; they're fanatical, yes, and some of the terrorists who took over the planes had degrees from universities. The real point is that from a young age they were schooled in the psychology of terrorism. But what's most scary is that they're more than willing to die for their cause.

I'm glad that what I've been telling people for years about the winning power of knowledge is slowly but surely showing signs of happening. We're finally getting important people in government with different philosophies about rushing into a war situation. Twenty-five years ago our government, without hesitation, would have bombed and invaded a country that very night; except for more dead bodies, the results would be, just like now, indecisive. The reason is that we're fighting a cause, not a country, and this cannot be won by having the biggest stick. The knowledgeable people in government who have learned from the pitfalls and dangers of overreacting and jumping into a bloody world war should be commended for commanding the restraint that kept us from making a big and costly mistake. For the sake of my grandchildren and yours, I hope there are a lot more of these people in the future.

Long before 9/11, I would remark to my family and friends how our own Toledo TV and newspaper were presenting a one-sided pro-Israel view on the hostilities between Israel and Palestine. The mainstream media put the bombing by Palestinians in Israel on the front page of the newspaper and the top story on TV news broadcast. They put the bombings and killing in refugee camps and the destroying of Palestinian towns by Israel on the second or third page of the paper and mentioned them only briefly on the news.

While the pro-Jewish media were preprogramming the American people with worn-out stories of oppressed Jews, three to four times as many Palestinians were dying compared to Israelis in the Israeli-Palestinian conflict.

People seeing the Holocaust programs on TV three or four times a week for the last four decades have been preprogrammed to and conditioned by a subliminal vision in their mind that the Jews are the only race that's ever been persecuted and were victims of genocide. Now we know it's happened to many others.

Here again, my main point is not about race; rather, it's about opening up one's mind and gaining knowledge as to who are the Puppeteers who orchestrate the "hate a race symphony." The everyday people are the ones to suffer and pay for these unnecessary wars. It makes no difference to the Puppeteers if you're circumcised or not. It's all about creating hate for the purpose of war, and the money to be made from it.

On the History Channel, you will see the German youth of World War II marching with guns. If you turn on the news today, you will see Israeli youth marching with guns. Why was one bad and the other good and necessary?

Our CIA and other government agencies knew about Bin Laden's involvement in the bombing of America's military installation and the bombing of the World Trade Center building in '93. Our government needs a Bin Laden, a Hussein, a Qadhafi, an Arafat, and so on, to keep our attention on violence and hate, and not on things of importance right here at home that our government is taking away from us.

Our billion-dollar satellite surveillance system must have been turned off when Bin Laden made TV broadcasts shortly after 9/11, traded stocks and had dealings with bankers. The worldwide media network knew where he was, but for some strange reason, our military didn't.

If the media had publicized the danger presented by the al-Qaeda terrorist cells in America, with the same emphasis before 9/11 as they did after, possibly the two buildings would still be standing.

• By scaring the American public into submission with the attack on America, paranoia can get the people to jump on the bandwagon for the media campaign for a new security system network. This will benefit the Pentagon and all the bureaucrats who get their hands on the billions of taxpayers' dollars. We will waste all this money changing what was supposed to be the best security system in the world *last year*. Frankly speaking, what good is a security system when the human beings monitoring it get orders to look the other way?

• Press secretary—speaks for the president—never been president.

• Military spokesman—speaks for the generals—never been a general.

• The befuddled American will get pissed off and ready to kill foreigners when the front page of the newspaper makes them the villain. Then turn to the sports page and praise a foreign athlete, because he helped their *home team* win.

• The media have been over-enthusiastic in reporting the troubles in the Catholic church. We've been fed a steady diet about the wrongdoings of some sick men (sorry, I mean priests). Why haven't we seen a story about the sexual perversion of a rabbi? After all, they're men.

• News analyst: a person who tells you what was just said. [Doesn't mean what you heard.]

• Paper + business X pen + politics X ink + word arrangers = newspaper.

• Paper of record: Puppeteers-controlled view.

• It would be refreshing to see a happy newspaper filled with nothing but happy news.

• "Freedom of the press" has the same double-standard meaning to the media as "The people have the right to know." The reason I haven't mentioned it before is that if I got started presenting my bartender's view on this term used by the media, it would end up being a book in itself.

Any puppet, including the CEO of a company, who ends up in an awkward situation will be out of the limelight and safe from public persecution by the Puppeteers-controlled media. The word arrangers will supply the disinformation and double-standard techniques to mislead the public. By the time the truth is told, the public will be busy watching the next TV circus, with their attitude being, "Ho-hum, so what? They all do it."

Media have distorted the truth throughout history, deliberately provoking crises to create a passion for war in the uninformed citizen's mind. We hope that soon the power of the media fits the adage, "It's going to be history, in the near future."

Chapter XI

THE BUSINESS OF WAR

"War, what is it good for? Nothing." Well, not exactly. It's for poor people killing other poor people, paying the ultimate price for the wealthy to get wealthier. The only winners in war are the Puppeteers; they write the scripts, direct, and produce the wars, but don't play in them.

America, in the last hundred years, has emerged as the world's most powerful country in the production of wars. We also went from being admired for our democracy to being feared and hated because of our government's "Big Stick" policy. Frankly speaking, in the future, I think that neither America nor any other nation will be capable of being the dominant controller of the world. One outstanding reason is that technology and communication make the world smaller.

From the Civil War to present-day wars, bankers who finance wars have made hundreds of millions of dollars, opening the bank vault for unlimited loans to produce the war machinery needed for any country's corrupt leaders (their puppets), whom history and the media will blame for starting it, knowing that when it's over, no matter what the results are, the countries involved will pay back the money borrowed, with interest. The loss of human life is not figured in their equations, just more millions that taxpayers blindly pay back. Americans should realize that money is spent for wars long before the mainstream media ever gives Americans a hint they're coming.

For years I've heard a statement used in America, a prepro-grammed acceptance of war that was subliminally planted in

Americans' heads by a system that makes war a business. "We have to have a war to pick up our economy." In other words, hating and killing to put money in our pockets is necessary for America's survival. War is deeply engraved in the American psyche—all's fair in love and war; this game is going to be a war; we declare war on poverty, illiteracy, crime, smoking, unemployment, obesity, terrorism, etc.

Serving and having conversation throughout the years with veterans of World War II, Korea, and Vietnam, along with friends and co-workers from these wars, I realized they all had one thing in common, besides loving America. Being older and wiser, they knew wars are presented with issues of phony, corrupt causes and the threat of losing our freedom; one of the biggest reasons for war is religion. In reality, the reasons they killed or wanted to kill other human beings were a lie to cover up the real truth that war is a business.

It will take a while until human beings are knowledgeable enough to realize that war is unnecessary. Until that happens, there will always be some preprogrammed psycho who likes to kill someone he doesn't know for someone else he doesn't know. Most combat vets I knew and read about who have seen the horrors of war would never go through it again. They saw things first-hand, and after all is said and done, killing another human is not an easy thing to live with.

There are too many "what ifs" in religion to kill over. The different views on which god is God has had everyday people, for centuries, going to war and killing other human beings who were preprogrammed just like them, for the same reason—to be used by the controllers as pawns in the business of war, by tricking them with religious beliefs for excuses to hate. Frankly speaking, if heaven is supposed to be so glorious, why do we wait so long to get there?

It's the low-mid Americans who make up the majority of people who die in American wars and have the most loved ones who never get over their loss. In the future, low-mid Americans could start deprogramming themselves by opening their heads and discovering how great it is to let your own thought processes sort things out, without a one-sided preprogrammed view to hate. Whose god is right, liberal, conservative, Republican, Democrat, right or left, union or non-union, white or non-white? All these "differences" infused in American society obscure judgment. Wars would not be easy to orchestrate if these and other preprogrammed reasons to hate or judge other human beings were decided by the individual's feeling, based on his or her own informed mindset.

Teach future generations the lessons learned through the previous mistakes of our money-motivated reasons for war; don't teach things like violence, revolutions using violence, violent government takeovers, hating just because the media wants you to—this kind of thinking is not the answer. Teaching them by pursuing different sources of information for judgment and decision-making on voting for our future leaders would be a good start to reduce the chance of unnecessary wars in the future. If future politicians knew they have to work for *us* (who?) and not for the soft-money contributors, all of our grandkids would have a brighter future. Because of preprogrammed reasons to hate, the potential strength of low-mid Americans as a voting block is being wasted. Instead of being at odds with each other, we should realize we're all in the same boat, getting screwed by the people we vote into office. To change our situation takes no more than breaking down the barriers in the brain that won't allow information in, because of preprogrammed prejudices and hate. Frankly speaking, the information revolution is in full swing. The answers are out there and all it takes is to break old habits stubbornly stuck in our brains, and take notice that people brown, yellow, and white are killing each for the color of green.

Now that the brutal reality of war has hit home, and is not just in someone else's back yard, maybe Americans will stop believing Puppeteer-controlled information outlets about whom to hate without knowing both sides of the problems. Now we stop depending on the puppet politicians who wave the banners of righteousness, freedom, truth, and honor, while at the time having their hands under the table collecting money from the military spending kickbacks to the war industry's lobbyists.

The reason for military spending is easily sold, yet there's no money for schools or helping the old. Our tax dollars are not being used to help us! They go to the Pentagon and end up in rust.

The Pentagon has become a front for the business of war. Investors and shares sold are not needed when a never-ending supply of tax dollars will all be available for the Pentagon corporation to maintain a successful business that depends on the marketing of their product, war. When war became subliminally accepted in Americans' mindset, it turned into a business. Most Americans are media-controlled onlookers, taking for granted that military spending is needed, no matter what the cost.

I'm not living in la-la land; I know military strength is still needed. But if more Americans put as much interest in how and where our tax dollars are wasted through Pentagon spending as they do in the Puppeteers-controlled media sideshows, the money wasted in corruption from manufacturers' overpricing to kickbacks from contractors, lobbyists and bureaucratic waste could be used instead to help America where the help is really needed.

We've been living through an era of investigation committees, independent counsels, senate hearing committees, and many more on corruption that result in nothing but a waste of money and a slap on the hand (closing the barn door after the livestock gets out).

A serious investigation into Pentagon spending practices could never get off the ground, unlike attacks on the Mafia, small business and big business outsiders, sports, gambling, unions, pornography, and drug cartels. The reason is that the puppets we hear and see doing the double talking and word arranging, if they don't do as they're told by the Puppeteers, jeopardize their money-making business. They get their purse strings cut off, and if that doesn't work, they might end up with more than their purse strings being cut off. (Keeping this business out of the red depends on people ending up dead.)

From Hitler to Hussein, the Puppeteers have put in and out of power, or let stay in power, egomaniacal rulers who are perfect for promoting hate. The sole purpose of these scapegoats is to justify the unlimited military spending for the business of war. Castro's Cuba has been claimed to be a threat from communism, and other Mickey Mouse reasons for us to worry about have been promoted for the last forty-some odd years. To me, that's like Iowa being a threat to the rest of the United States.

If economic pressure was sufficient to break down Russia and win the so-called Cold War, why does Iraq, or why did Cuba, pose a military threat to the U.S. that justifies war?

In the blink of an eye, our political process allocated $355 billion for upgrading our defense system and new weapons for war on terrorism, when we were supposed to have had the best in the world already. In comparison, we can't come up with a few extra dollars needed for our public schools; we're eliminating school programs and teachers with the lame excuse of inadequate budget. Education can't compete with war for tax dollars. The most important occupation for future generations, teaching, doesn't have the importance or priority as the Pentagon's spending hundreds of millions of dollars on more weapons for Israel.

Israel has all the latest military toys the Pentagon can send them, and they still can't stop suicide bombers because they're dealing with defeating a cause. A able solution is the only solution, not $355 billion going to the Pentagon for the business of war. Frankly speaking, if the draft could be eliminated, as well as military spending, then with the state lottery system, there would be enough money for our children to have individual tutors.

When American settlers pushed American Indians off their land, the government word arrangers' one-sided version went down as history, making the heathen savage wrong and the Christianity holier-than-thou version right. I'm not worried if there are still people in America who believe this was the truth, and that we were morally right; they won't be reading this book.

I wondered earlier how Americans would react if the American Indians had a financial and military power, with a bigger stick than the U.S., to back them today, and would start kicking Americans off the land that belonged to the Indians two or three hundred years ago. Because we would be out-gunned, Americans would have to fight back with the same tactics we used before in history, when the British called us ter-rorists.

For a century and a half, Americans unknowingly have been consumers of information that only went to parts of the brain that the knowledge producers have fertilized with disinforma-tion on the reasons for war.

Disinformation and a one-sided, not-to-question version about "Israel's War" has Americans in a state of fear, worrying whether they'll get blown up or end up with some germ that was intentionally distributed while they are conducting everyday, routine activities.

The fear of being labeled "anti-Semitic" has most news sources reporting the Israeli interpretation of events in Palestine, accepted without question. Again, this is not about hating Jews, but just a few things that I have noticed and wanted to point out with no malice intended to those who belong to a nationality. It's just my view, based on the facts at hand.

• When Israel is hit by a Palestinian bomber and women and children are killed, it will be on the front page of the news-paper and the top story on the newscast. When Israel bombs a city in Palestine and kills women and children, you will find the story somewhere in the middle of the newspaper and maybe briefly mentioned on the newscast.

I don't know of any country in the world our government and media would condone as we do Israel's aggressive actions, like shooting rockets into refugee camps filled with innocent people because someone thinks terrorists might be there, and tanks smashing down homes because someone has an inkling that terrorists might be in them. These are brown-shirt tactics.

• There was a media blitz of time and money for the prose-cution of the people responsible for the death of a Jewish reporter who took a gamble on corralling a big story and lost, but there was little media attention about prosecuting the people responsible for killing a dedicated American lady, Dian Fossey, who was hacked to death by poachers in Africa.

• How come an American who goes to Israel to fight for his religious cause is not labeled by the media, while another American (before 9/11) who went to support his religious cause in Afghanistan is called a traitor by the media? I guess the media decide what religious freedom is.

• How different the reporting would have been if it were the Vatican that was shelled and not the Church of the Nativity.

In every bar I ever worked or spent time in, there was always a small, big-mouthed, pushy troublemaker who hung with a big, powerful man who would back him up when his mouth overloaded his ass. This reminds me of Israel's bullying tactics, used only because they have their big buddy, the U.S. government, to back them.

There's another factor in the "Israel is right" version that the mainstream media, TV, and Hollywood movie industries' word arrangers have been presenting to America. It's hard not to be one-sided when 80 percent of the top-brass decision makers are Jewish. (To go into more detail on this would take another book). I have openly talked with Jewish people on this subject without an anti-Semitic atmosphere and most have agreed with me on who controlled the news and entertainment business. As far as I'm concerned the facts would be the same, no matter what nationality it was.

A few years ago, on the Emmys, one of the award presenters said, "A gay woman in a man's suit surrounded by Jews will really piss the Taliban off." The audience stood and gave her a tremendous applause.

Back in 1949 or 1950, my mother let the Jewish neighbors talk her into letting them watch *The Goldbergs* on TV. But when they asked her to watch the Oscars, she would say, "I'm not going to watch a bunch of Jews pass out trophies to each other." (The same as always.)

Frankly speaking, the war with Iraq and backing Israel in reality is all about land, not religion, and the power and wealth (oil) it yields.

The question is: How much longer will American taxpayers be able to afford paying for arms the Pentagon sends to Israel in their land-grabbing quest—oops, that's right, they're called settlers.

Before the first Iraq war games in the early nineties, a military spokesman on TV was trying to make it look to the American public like Iraq was a military threat, stating that Iraq was the third or fourth best-equipped military in the world. That was beyond a bunch of bull; it was the next thing to outright lying. They were equipped with our leftover, hand-me-down weapons from Vietnam. They couldn't even defeat Iran with our help. (Yesterday's allies, today's enemies.) The real proof that they were no threat was the end result. They weren't even in the game. Hussein was left in power by our government to be used again for military spending in the business of war.

While speaking on TV at one of the war pep rallies (presidential press conferences), our head puppet was blaming Hussein for using nerve gas on his own people, calling this the use of weapons of mass destruction. I guess his word-arrangers forgot that our government used nerve gas on our own people in Waco. Another time in a speech, he said, "We won't tolerate any country that breaks a treaty." Again, someone seems to have forgotten about our treaties with the American Indians.

Remorse is a strong human emotion. Our desire to respect the deceased is a human tendency that is used against us for monetary gain.

Like price-gouging done by morticians, to emotionally weak people after the deaths of loved ones, our Pentagon dishes out large sums of taxpayers' money (with the help of lobbyists) to dig up bones of American soldiers that are scattered around on some island where a World War II battle took place, using the remorse as a cover-up for military spending.

If the relatives of these soldiers were given a choice to use the money for a few sixty-year-old bones or to use it constructively in their own community, I think most would choose the latter, but no, the business of war won't allow that to happen.

As the quote says, "Perhaps it is a universal truth that the loss of liberty at home is to be charged to provision against danger, real or pretended, from abroad."

The Homeland Security Act (HSA) will be remembered as the government's attack on America's homeland. For one thing, it's too late; the terrorists are already here (this will have the same effect as a condom has on eliminating AIDS). Frankly, the HSA will prove detrimental to our freedom. What's hidden in the fine print of the act is more government control, resulting in American citizens losing more rights. The word-arrangers use preventing terrorism as an ulterior motive for using brown-shirt tactics in our ever-rising police state atmosphere.

Pushing a national identity card down our throats will put more strain on Americans' already diminishing privacy. Illegal phone taps, breaking down doors without court orders, not to mention IRS investigations, will become commonplace, causing American citizens to spend more of their hard-earned cash defending themselves, with the money going into the already fat pockets of the legal profession. The HSA will enable the government to put more leverage on the gun-control issue that should be a non-issue.

Throughout the years, I've watched whenever an issue would benefit our government, but not the people as a whole, how our government uses special-interest groups' opinions on an issue as the majority opinion.

Our Constitution is being dismantled every day while Americans are looking the other way. The HSA is going to make it worse, that's for sure. One important essential freedom is the Second Amendment. To me and millions of other Americans, it's more than the "Saturday-night special" controversy. Passing gun control laws will not stop people from having guns; it will only make it illegal and costly. It's asinine to think a written law will be able to keep a criminal from getting a gun. They tried it in England and all it accomplished was to give the advantage to the criminal, making crimes perpetrated against citizens skyrocket.

Myself and three-fourths of low-mid America have been raised with a gun in the home environment. Accidental deaths resulting from gun accidents in the home were, and still are, few and far between, compared to the total number of homes with a gun. It would be great if the enormous negative publicity targeted toward the few accidents would be channeled toward reducing the production of violent video games that market gruesome dismemberment, blood, and gore, presenting death as a game to the young.

The special-interest groups and pro-gun-control lobbyists are taking a few mishaps and a few mixed-up youths to make gun control a major, right-now issue (along with the help of the media, with the blessing of our government). If they really cared about the young, they wouldn't allow manufacturers to produce and sell cars with big, powerful engines that produce speeds twice the legal limit that kill more of our youth than guns ever will, except in war.

What gun control will do is allow the criminal to have a field day taking advantage of unarmed citizens who trusted the government to protect them. As long as guns are manufactured, the "lowlifes" will be able to get one. The legal profession already has made it possible for the criminal to have more rights than the victim. The fear of being shot while invading a home is more of a deterrent than going to jail and lifting weights, watching TV, or suing the government (us taxpayers) because the criminals' rights are being violated will ever be.

"Them God damn foreigners." I must have heard this a thousand times as a young boy, years later in the factory and behind the bar and elsewhere in life. I've heard this statement roll off people's tongues, totally forgetting about their own heritage; being so preprogrammed with hate, most do not think about being descendants of immigrants. Descendants of what are now the main nationalities that make up America were foreigners or slaves at one time in history, with most having come here for opportunity or the better way of life that freedom provides (and that still holds true). But in reality, the biggest share of immigrants that were sold "the streets paved with gold" story, were brought here to be a workforce for the conglomerates of industry.

For decades, flooding America with immigrants to be used for labor was the aim of early American conglomerates. They're still used for cheap labor, but now they're called "aliens" and serve another purpose: to keep Americans hating each other over diversity among nationalities, religions, and color, at the same time we are occupied hating outsiders. The Puppeteers use their puppets to rearrange our Constitution and devise ways to infringe on the freedom that is the heart and soul of America's greatness.

Frankly speaking, coming to America, becoming a citizen, and enjoying our freedom is not the problem. The problem is people that come here to kill American citizens and destroy our freedom.

While the public attention is diverted debating and hating what's on the front page, blaming agents of the CIA, FBI, and INS for 9/11, the decision-makers of these organizations and the administrators they report to who sat on the information for political reasons are infighting within their organization or told to look the other way.

Frankly, the buck stops here, NSA (National Security Agency). If this puppet doesn't use or get all the information from the heads of the NIS, FBI, and CIA regarding the safety of America, what the hell good are they then? Another organization or business could not function properly and their top decision-maker would be removed (fired) if they blew a call like 9/11.

The word arrangers' headlines detour our thought process, preprogramming people with their handpicked stories on what's important, the old sleight-of-hand ploy, and diverting you with the left hand while the right hand goes unnoticed. Planting seeds of hate with disinformation makes the business of war escalate.

LEFT HAND—Saber rattling speeches calling Korea part of the axis of evil (in reality Korea and Iraq have more differences than similarities). RIGHT HAND—Letting Enron officials who ripped off investors of millions, after a terrible scolding, slide out the back door (as everybody should know by now, through connections with the Bush administration).

LEFT HAND—Inducing phone surveys with the help of media hype to get people to call in their opinion on a no-brainer question. Should McDonald's be sued by parents because the parents let their child get obese by gorging himself on fat-burgers and fries? RIGHT HAND—Phone companies working their marketing scheme to generate more revenue spurned by the new American craze, the cell phone, tricking people into wasting money thinking their opinion means something.

Thanks to the information revolution produced by the computer, we are right around the corner from being able to break free from being preprogrammed disinformation consumers of the Puppeteers' money-motivated reasons for killing people we don't even know for the business of war.

I don't know how many times since the late sixties up to the present after commenting behind the bar, at work, or at a party on the discrepancy between what I read and what the mainstream media was selling to the American public about the ongoing war, a doubting Thomas would pop up and say, "Just because you read it in a book, doesn't make it so." My reply would be, "Books, not book, and other sources outside the newspaper, *Newsweek*, and TV newscast sources of information." I always felt confident in my view; it was obtained through my thirst for the truth and reading both sides of the spectrum, or else I wouldn't take a stand on the subject.

My mother always stressed the value of finishing every book I read; also, the old quote "know your enemies" has made my view on a subject usually hold water.

Four decades, watching the big picture has been like watching a long-running miniseries written and produced by the Puppeteers. They replace information with disinformation, allowing them to control information to set the plot, in turn making it easy to mislead people into blaming who or what they want blamed, not who or what should be blamed.

After the money spent and lives lost, nothing was attained, nothing was achieved that benefited low-mid Americans in the past fifty years of being in and out of wars. War should be a last resort and the military a deterrent, not a human resource used for financial gain. We have the intelligence to create smart bombs, but not the wisdom to see they're unnecessary.

Regardless of the word arrangers' justification for a war, such as keeping our freedom intact (never a threat, like it is right now from the provisions in the Homeland Security Act), stopping the flow of drugs, defeating communism (whatever the hell that is), protecting human rights when it's financially beneficial, terrorism, oilism, low-mid Americans wind up paying more taxes for the business of war.

There used to be some consolation in the fact that more low-mid working-class Americans were employed making military products. Now most of the materials are manufactured in cheap-labor countries by the same American conglomerates, so they can stuff a larger portion of our tax dollar into their already bulging pockets.

In the aftermath of wars, the perpetrators of war crimes, the madmen who were allowed to invade some helpless country, and the evil regimes are ridiculed and condemned by the media and prosecuted by our government as criminals.

When are the financial institutions that provide the money and profit for the loans held accountable for their part in destruction and death? How come the most powerful government in the world can't make financial institutions tell where Bin Laden is? They can't move his money around without knowing where he is.

Hitler was portrayed as an uncontrollable madman who wanted to control the world. If he was uncontrollable, why didn't he invade Switzerland where the wealth of the world is stored, with no army to speak of? Probably afraid of their weapon of mass destruction, the Swiss army knife.

I'm a grandfather against war and proud of it. History has brought to light that every war in the last sixty years was never caused by who or what was on the front page that let America into a war. To help with the deception, the president will back up the media with a pro-war speech brewed up by his advisors who are controlled by the Puppeteers, who make a killing off war's killings.

Frankly speaking, I believe it's unpatriotic not to speak out against corruption and wrongdoings by presidents or any other politicians and government officials.

If there are any questions about my love of America and my appreciation and admiration for men and women in the military, they would be put to rest if you knew how I get goose bumps when the national anthem is sung. Especially when sung so beautifully before the Red Wings' home games. (Thank you, Karen.)

There are a lot of Americans who feel about war like I do; too bad there are too many who don't.

Chapter XII

DRINK FOR THOUGHT

Gays

Gay bars have been around longer than I, and will be around long after I'm gone. It's part of the bar business. After tending bar and being in heterosexual bars all my life, I found that gays frequent heterosexual establishments for the same reasons straight people do: to enjoy the nightlife, have a few drinks, dance, talk, and if they're lucky, get lucky.

The gay customers I have known throughout the years were never a problem; most were nice, easygoing people, clean, polite, and better than average spenders, usually with a good income. Frankly speaking, homosexuality is an individual's right and freedom to exercise. The sexual preference of gays should be accepted, not sensationalized.

Rubbing elbows with people from both sides of the tracks, one thing I've noticed is that the violence among homosexuals is a mirror image of the violence in our society overall. Knowledgeable, educated gays don't display the vicious violence in their lovers' spats that gays from the uneducated lower side of the tracks do.

A long time ago, in a nightclub, I was trying to hit on a gorgeous lady. Just when I got to first base, her companion sat down at the table. After a "Hi, how are you?" he-she lifted her shirt up to show me the gun tucked in her belt. She gave her little bambi a wet one, and grinned at me like a shark to make sure I got the picture, and I certainly did.

From this and other experiences, I believe male homosexuals (other than a few incidences) don't have the same level of intensity in their jealousy involving their lovers as the hardcore lesbians' violent over-protectiveness. Just a guess, maybe it's due to the femininity in the fellas and the masculinity in the he-shes. Homosexuality is still one of the unanswered questions in nature that will be understood with more time and knowledge. That is, when we start using more of our time to obtain knowledge. The impact of special-interest groups in the political arena and media makes controversy more of a factor than logic.

I don't think we should be force-fed the idea that homosexuality is normal. If it were normal, how the hell did mankind survive and flourish? Allowing for the possibility that something might change drastically in our future, human beings, like all species on Earth, were meant to reproduce. If it were normal for men to make it with men, and women with women, I wouldn't be here to write this and you wouldn't be here to read it. Frankly speaking, gay people who need to obtain notoriety about being gay have a bigger problem than their sexuality.

I would never put homosexuals in a category of the street fags who sell their bodies for dope. People of this kind usually have deep mental problems caused by something in their past that produced a distorted outlook for the future. Male bisexuals are screwed up individuals who don't know what they want or who they are. Married bisexuals who cheat on their wives are in a category of their own, one that I can't come up with a description for.

The overnight changing of laws by our legislators to accommodate gays, in order to capture the vote of the gay voting block, is extending our meaning of freedom and not trusting the laws of simple logic. For people to be in love, no matter what gender is involved, is an individual right, but I think that gay couples adopting and raising children is wrong. The raising of children is tougher now than ever. When gays adopt children, they're thinking too much about their own well-being, and not taking into consideration how it will affect a young person growing up in today's society. It's hard enough for adolescents without giving unnecessary fire power for verbal abuse by other children, with remarks like, "Which one is your dad or mom?" "Who gets on top?" or "Your parents are freaks," and a lot worse with today's standards as they are. The chance of normality for a child having to grow up in this situation won't be as good as the chance of becoming an introverted head case, or a cold, mentally tough person with a chip on his shoulder.

Gay bashing is just another part of our violent times that media can sensationalize to keep the violent mindset implanted in our society. Gay bashing is done by weak-minded macho males who get their jollies by inflicting pain on someone when the odds are in their favor. For the media, the gay subject is a great tool to stir up controversy to create hate and anger, with no intention of helping gays, but to keep us looking the other way while the serious problems for America's future are being perpetrated with the hope of someday making front-page news of problems after the damage is done.

Gays have good acting skills. Maybe it's because of having to put on an act most of their lives. Hollywood has always been a sanctuary for gays; it's no secret that a good share of the entertainment industry is gay. There's hardly a movie made these days without a gay character popping up in it somewhere.

The influential Hollywood gay crowd is subliminally putting the idea in young people's minds that gays are normal, with their word-arrangers writing movie scripts that confuse and mislead the highly impressionable youth of today. Hollywood is not giving young people a chance to grow up and make their own decisions with their own feelings on sexuality.

Favorite lame question asked by gay rights activists whenever a heterosexual gets an attitude about not wanting to be gay: "What's the matter, are you insecure about your own sexuality?"

The Hollywood press agents are the Merlins of the entertainment industry. By making a rumor into the truth, and truth into a rumor, they magically get the movie-minded public to accept anything they promote as acceptable. If you're a money-making star, and get caught in a gay love affair, the Hollywood Merlin will market a story that you're not gay, but bisexual. The preprogrammed movie public will fall for this sleight of hand and tell themselves, "I guess it's all right."

A gay female couple, with one of them being a big recording star, decided to have a baby and one of them would be artificially inseminated. For the father, they picked another well-known recording star. When the entertainment Merlins got done sugar-coating it with superlatives, not only was it accepted, but some thought it was cool. This couple was thinking as much about publicity for their cause as they were about having a baby. No offense to the male recording star they picked; I think he's a great artist. But if they were thinking of their baby's health, I don't know why they would choose someone with a history of liver problems and drug overdoses, and someone in poor physical shape to be a father.

Frankly speaking, I guess my preprogrammed old-fashioned ideas are hard to overcome sometimes, but I still think it is better for all concerned to keep homosexuality behind closed doors for a while, if only because of kids. I believe as time goes by we will gain the knowledge to open the door.

Road Rage

When you combine ignorance with the anger pent up in today's inconsiderate, hurry-up society, throw in an automobile, and you have the basic elements for road rage. The stress level of the American people is at an all-time high, and nowhere is it more evident than behind the wheel of a car. In the last twenty years, what has happened on the road reflects the way people are growing up indignant, with no manners or respect, just attitude. "Screw everyone else, I'm in a hurry."

Because of our pressure-cooker lifestyle, drivers get behind the wheel all stressed out, and vent their anger toward strangers, usually for all the wrong reasons: spent too much time in front of the mirror, fought with the other half, pissed at the boss, impatient after looking at miles of orange barrels in a traffic jam, "Someone cut me off yesterday, so I'll cut this guy off today." People work themselves into emotional madness and want to hurt someone over a couple of minutes of valuable time. Not until it's too late do people realize they have in their hands a weapon that can put them in a life-or-death situation in a heartbeat. And, chances are, the person in the other car has the same mindset.

People always get mad at inconsiderate and rude drivers on the road. You might have given them the finger or laid on the horn to let them know they were wrong, but very seldom did it escalate into the brain-dead violence like today. People used to tolerate such mistakes, which we all have committed. Why not use a little discretion and back off? Be a little humble and don't be a punk with an attitude.

Quite often a customer would come through the door saying, "Frank, pour me a stiff one, I need it bad. Some asshole just cut me off," or describe some other white-knuckle driving experience they would be upset about. After a drink or two, they would calm down and forget it. Those were the good old days. Every now and again there might have been a physical altercation, but people didn't take it so personal.

Today in our hurry-up, get-ahead, capitalistic, time-is-money mindset, people find it too easy to jump into the part of the brain where hate lives. With our acceptance of violence and uptight frame of mind, people take another person's driving mistake personally and work themselves into a rage, wanting to scrutinize and brutalize someone over the same thing they did yesterday, with the end result being higher insurance premiums and more money in judicial pockets.

I think relaxing with a drink or two after a tough day helps relieve some pent-up stress and will, maybe, keep you from overreacting to someone's no-brainer on our overcrowded roadways. I'm not promoting getting hammered and getting behind the wheel, but for some people, taking the edge off helps a little. I know a bunch of do-gooders won't understand this, so have another doctor prescribe Valium and relax, and don't take it personally.

It was a lot easier to control my temper when handling drunken assholes as a bartender than controlling it dealing with today's drivers. Frankly speaking, the yellow caution traffic light in today's "I'm late" world means hurry up and floor it, even if you're a hundred feet away from the intersection, and throw caution to the wind.

The inconsiderate attitude that's exhibited on the road is also evident in other areas in today's "me first, who cares, everybody else does it, don't get involved, screw you," uptight, non-compassionate society. (If being considerate and respectful is absent in older people, how can we expect youngsters to be considerate and respectful?)

Parents

It starts at home. The family is the cornerstone of society. As the years went by, the age gap between bar customers and myself began to grow. Not only did they become younger, but disrespectful; mannerless, inconsiderate, know-it-all customers grew in numbers at the same time that more parents began telling me their woes about losing touch with their uncontrollable children.

Parents in the seventies and eighties started raising children with the advice given to them in books by so-called experts. Books by Dr. Shock and Dr. Mothers were publicized by the multiple-tentacle marketing system that sold the idea to young parents not to spank or scold their children or they would grow up to be maladjusted, scared, etc. The backlash from the teaching of these books shows in most young adults in today's society. They don't know the value of perseverance, dedication, patience, self-reliance, all very important character builders; family traits of common courtesy such as saying "please," "thank you," "excuse me," "pardon" are uncommon in most young adults' "who cares" mindset of today. (Childcare belongs to ma and dad, not daycare centers.)

Frankly speaking, beating a child often or brutally is wrong, but a slap on a toddler's hand or butt never mentally harmed a child. My children don't ever remember being spanked, but do remember the tone in my voice.

During the off nights in the bar business you usually got into some interesting chit-chat with a few of the regular customers. When the controversy on disciplining children would be the topic, I had a theory I used to lay on my customers and friends. If back in the caveman days a commanding, loud voice by parents directed at children hadn't been effective, humans might not have made it.

Just imagine this scene: The father is a hundred feet away from the front of the cave, working and gathering for their everyday survival. The family is hanging out in front of the cave. All of a sudden, Dad sees a wild animal sneaking up on his family. A short, resounding vocal command, and the family runs for safety. If it were today's Dr. and Dr. books mindset, you would say, "Now kids, I don't want to yell at you, but ..." They would have been long gone, ending up in some animal's stomach. Protecting and caring is love, which is much more important than some doctor's psychological bull-crap that's used for marketing. From cavemen to the modern family, children not only need discipline as they grow older but also need to realize you really care.

If parents today would tell their children what my mother used to say to me—"Until you pay the bills around here, you do as I say. Straight up to your room and no supper"—they would end up in court for child abuse; our legal system would make sure of it.

When punishing a child, having a guilt trip afterwards is unnecessary if good intention was the motive. I knew women I worked with in bars and in my personal life whose "old man" was a lowlife and didn't have anything to do with the kids after the divorce; these women would be on a guilt trip and be afraid to take on the responsibility of parenthood. Feeling sorry for their children not having a father in their lives, they let their children control them and do whatever they wanted. I would warn them: Giving and giving and responding to every gimme-gimme is not love, but being weak and ducking reality. We're raising children to become adults, and in the adult world nothing is free.

Mothers who didn't change their thinking stayed weak, and ended up with children who had to get married or knocked somebody up or got into drugs and crime before they had a chance to enjoy life. Another weakness they had was that when they did punish children they would turn right around and reward them because of guilt. You don't wait until they're teens to establish respect and control. Those teenagers in Columbine, Colorado, who shot up that school are a good example. What shocked me was the parents' attitude. One of their lame excuses was, "He didn't allow us in his room." Kids making their own rules and parents going along with it has become commonplace.

The movie and TV industries use their marketing word-arrangers to show kids laughing at and making fun of their parents, teens being "smarter" than their parents, children dictating to their parents on their wants and needs, by making it all look cool. They marketed disrespect and no need for discipline and turned kids into "I got to have it" spenders of their parents' money. Parents letting this happen is one of the major reasons for the need for a two-income family, to buy the novelty items and fashions that end up in the back of the closet or in a garage sale next year.

Kids today don't care if it's new or fashionable or workable; all they care about is the logo, label, or symbol that the entertainment industry is marketing with celebrities. Parents let their kids convince them that they gotta have it or else. Everybody has one; if they don't, they will be picked on and made fun of. Parents let their kids fall prey to peer pressure, thinking it reflects on them personally, instead of teaching them that material things don't make a person.

Frankly speaking, we never got our children all the items on their list of wants, and we're proud that they didn't grow up to be a "handful of take and a mouthful of gimme."

Customers became friends and friends became customers. As a bartender, I had the opportunity to watch parents and their children grow up. There have been quite a few moms and dads who sat in front of me pounding alcohol, not enjoying life, full of doubts, whipping themselves, complaining about their failure as parents. I was in the same boat myself for a while.

After years of listening to stories from every angle and reading books in psychology and personal development, I realized there's no such thing as a perfect parent (my children will testify to that). Making mistakes while raising children is as inevitable as in any other part of life.

That's why grandparents are important to grandchildren: "We've been there, done that; we can make the mistakes of mom, dad, or the grandchild more acceptable by presenting them in a different light." Years back, I saw a bumper sticker on a car that read, "If I would have known grandkids were this much fun, I would have had them first."

It's natural for most lower-middle-class parents to want their kids to have more than they did. The marketing network took that weakness and used it against parents by using every method in their arsenal to show kids how to turn the screws on their parents with the "I got to have it" ploy, knowing parents will spend, spend, spend.

Parents are using a big share of their income pacifying their children with things that in a matter of months will no longer be cool, or will end up in a garage sale next year. They also use up a lot of their time shopping around for those (so-called) important needs, like running to the carry-out between TV commercials to get junk food, taking them to and picking them up from the mall for no special reason except to hang out, having to pick them up when they're three blocks away because they won't walk that far. Cell phones and personal TVs for grade-schoolers are spoiling children and teaching them bad habits. Parents could use that money for genuine needs and better purposes. Raising children today has made a one-car family almost obsolete, and two cars in a family not enough sometimes. The Puppeteers and their puppets love the way parents have been brainwashed into trying to be the "perfect parent."

With love as a motivator and guide, if parents can instill discipline, respect, and a good dose of manners in children, both parents and children will never regret it. To me, that's about as close to being a perfect parent as it gets.

I don't believe parents caught up in the pressures of survival, to the point of being stressed out, can or should stop what they're doing to explain to a two-year-old why they're being told "No." I have never talked to anyone who remembers why their parents told them "No" when they were two years old.

Young people who are parents should not let themselves be preprogrammed by a marketing system where the welfare of the family isn't as important as the bottom line of a financial report, and keeps them from using their own inclinations about what's common sense, right or wrong regarding their own or their children's happiness.

Because of a college degree, social workers who are in their mid twenties, not married, having no children, advise parents about rights and wrongs of parenthood. That's like a bartender telling a chef what spices he should use. Family valuables have become more important than family values. Parents are pre-programmed into putting so much effort into providing a financially secure future for their children instead of providing the little everyday things that can make their adult life less of a financial strain. Turn lights off when leaving a room, don't leave water running while you're doing something else, use your head instead of calculators all the time, do not be a twenty-first-century waste freak. All tips that will make their children's future more rewarding (and also help preserve natural resources) are within a parent's grasp. Some parents actually believe they're expressing love for their children by letting kids make their own decisions on their wants and needs. It's not fair to their children.

The young adults I have known who grew up thinking "I should get whatever I want" were controllers, one-sided, moody, and, as hard as they tried not to show it, were insecure. Another dismal result I've noticed that runs pretty true to form, is that these people don't have lifelong friends. The older you get, the wonderful feeling you get from lifelong friends is priceless.

Frankly speaking, regardless of their educational status, parents are more knowledgable than their children. It's too bad there're so many who don't know that important point.

It's unheard of for a teen not to have discontent and some rebelliousness, regardless of the best effort by parents. After all, didn't we all have the urge to do what we weren't supposed to do when we were young? When my daughter was going through the turbulent teens, I used to tell her, "If you look in the mirror, and don't like yourself, call Dad," the person in whom she always saw love and trust.

I wasn't as good a parent as I could have been, but I can honestly say that caring for the well-being of my children has never left me. And no one could have had a better mother for their children than my ex-wife, Elaine.

Bar Laws

In Toledo and across the nation, there has been a lot of attention focused on the no-smoking issue. As I mentioned earlier, nicotine and alcohol go hand in hand in the bar and nightclub business. You're not forced to go into a bar or nightclub. Anyone who enters a bar or nightclub has to know there will be people smoking. Until they quit making cigarettes, there won't be a change in this worldwide habit anytime soon.

Because of a bunch of do-gooders who have the media and insurance companies on their side, now we have to hurry up, change laws, and add more regulations to our already over-regulated life, when the issue can be solved with a commonsense solution, such as a simple sign in the window: Smoking or No Smoking. Freedom of choice is what America is all about. (From friends to customers that I have known, when out having a few drinks, they would occasionally smoke.)

When the media gets gung-ho over an issue, it's because nine out of ten times, somewhere down the line, it will benefit the Puppeteers. Frankly speaking, I see it as a way for the alcohol industry and the insurance companies, who are part of the Puppeteers' network, to eliminate another Ma and Pa neighborhood business by adding more regulations and laws that lead to higher operating expenses, just as they made it financially impossible for other Ma and Pa neighborhood businesses to survive, such as grocery stores, drug stores, small retail stores, and gas stations.

On this simple issue, the real smoke is being blown by the legal profession and lobbyists of the alcohol industry and insurance companies as well as the Puppeteers' main weapon, the

media, who will get all the preprogrammed do-gooders to do
their dirty work for them. Insurance companies will sell new
policies with higher premiums that will create more revenue. A
handful of big companies will monopolize and control another
major consumer business. (I guess they don't use the word
"monopoly" anymore; now they're called "mergers.")

Frankly, I have to ask: Why do we have laws and regulations that make something wrong or illegal, when it's not illegal
to manufacture or sell it? Things like nicotine, alcohol, guns,
and cars that are made to go twice as fast as the legal speed
limit—these are just some of the double-standard items that
keep the legal industry rich and in control.

Frankly speaking, if it could be proven that secondhand
smoke kills healthy people, the legal profession would have
been reaping the harvest with lawsuits long ago. If a person has
an existing condition of respiratory problems, yes, it is dangerous. But I don't consider nightclubs and bars public places. A
bartender has the right to refuse to serve whoever he wants;
children are not allowed, unless accompanied by a grownup.

The low-mid working people, the majority of the regular
customers and the owner's lifeline in the neighborhood bar
business, are smokers. If a no-smoking law in bars is passed, a
lot of owners will have to let the regulars smoke, or they'll be
out of business; after the lawyers hit them with lawsuits and
state liquor agents come down on them, it will just be a matter
of time before the neighborhood bar owner's livelihood is
gone.

The nonsmokers or even the ex-smokers don't sit around
the bar bitching about people smoking. They know it's their
choice to walk through that door. It's people who don't even
go into a neighborhood bar who are doing all the bitching. I
don't think bars and nightclubs should be classified as places
the general public frequents. (Nobody is dragged *into* a bar,
though I've dragged a few out.)

Frankly speaking, exhaust fumes from cars, artificial
hormones, chemicals, preservatives in food, fast-food burgers
with more grease and filler than meat are health hazards that
secondhand smoke can't hold a flame to; these are health

hazards that the American public has to tolerate everyday. Why isn't the negative view that's used on a problem that can be solved with simple logic publicized with the same gusto toward the food industry, oil companies, and automobile manufacturers? The Puppeteers won't let that happen.

In the over-regulated bar business and lawsuit mindset of this era, bars and nightclubs have to make sure their employees are aware of mistakes that can cost owners their license and a lot more. But no matter how knowledgeable your staff is, there will still be a slip-up on occasion.

My good friend Kip, whom I've known for thirty years, and bartended with for some of that time, is one of the biggest nightclub owners in Toledo and knows the business as well as anyone. I know first-hand how adamant he is about the rules against serving drunks when training managers and staff. Also, Kip is very thorough when explaining the dos and don'ts of handling drunks and rowdy customers. But right now he has on his desk at least half a dozen lawsuits, and who knows how many other violations. I could put my grandchildren through college with the lawyer fees and legal costs of just the phony lawsuits that he has dealt with in the last decade, mostly due to our double-standard legal system, which survives and prospers by making new laws and regulations.

The state liquor agents or the vice cops can bust Kip or any other bar owner whenever they get the urge. All the new laws and regulations have made it so easy for them; it's like catching fish in a barrel.

Our legal and judicial word-arrangers, with the help of the media, have the public thinking it's done for the good of the people, when in reality it's about more ways for control and keeping the money pouring in. Every good-sized city works the same way, different owners backing different politicians. If your person is in office, the vice cops and state boys look the other way. If your person is not in office, you'll be at their mercy whenever they want to burn you.

If the agent or vice cop can't get lucky to be on the spot when an employee makes a human error, they will use entrapment techniques to get the job done. For reasons from promotion to quotas to politics, these people who are supposed to enforce the law will break the law. I know for a fact that one of their favorite methods is to send in a teen with a fake ID. It's not luck that they can pick out the one person with a fake ID in a crowded nightclub, then bust a bartender or waitress who's working their butts off dealing with hoards of customers. I know it's the responsibility of owners, managers, and employees to control under-age drinking, and most bars and nightclubs do a very good job and stay on top of the problem, but it's next to impossible for a bartender or waitress to catch everything. Try watching ten people you just served and the ten new ones you're about to serve, blending into a crowd of a hundred or more. Throw in being tired from working two jobs and, like most people do when working, thinking about your everyday problems and responsibilities; anyone in this situation is liable to make a mistake once in a while, just like most people do. The difference is that here they can go to jail or get sued. Considering all the factors bar and nightclub employees deal with, they do a good job; only a very small percentage of customers get away with anything. Young people have more time and opportunity to contrive a scheme to get a friend a drink than the employee has to catch all the goings-on in a busy club. (Like it was when I was young, it's all about the thrill of getting away with it, and you keep trying until you do.)

When it comes to being accountable for the customers after they have left the bar and ended up in an accident or charged with drunk driving, that can be loaded with variations of judgment calls for bar employees. What most people don't realize are the intangibles and the difficulty in making these decisions that you have to be responsible for.

It's hard to read the consumption level of some customers, unless you have years of experience (a rookie employee might not catch it right away). Some customers may have had, in the car, a bottle they finished before they walked through the door. It's possible for them to be served a drink or so before it's obvious that they're drunk. Some customers lie and say they're not driving or someone else is, so they can get the benefit of the doubt on how many is too many. Some might come from another bar or party where they got loaded before they even came to your club. Whether or not you served them, because your bar was the last place they were, the police and ambulance chasers put you at fault.

When drunks get in an accident and don't mention being in a bar, or the police don't know they were in a bar, you won't hear too much about it. But if a drunk is coming from a bar, then it's newsworthy. If it's an accident in which death or severe injuries occur, the ambulance chasers will have a lawsuit on the bar owner's desk as quickly as possible, blaming the bar owners for something that wasn't their fault. Hitting people with lawsuits is very lucrative for the legal profession, win or lose.

I know there are establishments that don't give a damn about the welfare of the customer, but the majority of bars and nightclubs are careful not to let a drunk get on the road. Frankly speaking, it's not as easy as most people might think.

I've tended bar at private parties where judges, lawyers, politicians, and other influential people would leave shit-faced drunk and drive. I overheard conversations of these upstanding, law-abiding citizens, bragging about not getting a ticket when stopped after the last party they left drunk.

I tended bar at a fundraiser years back, at the home of a powerful legal person. Ninety percent of the guests were from the legal profession and politics. After leaving the party drunk, one of the word-arrangers was responsible for a serious-injury accident and charged with drunk driving. He didn't sue Mister Big for getting him drunk and letting him drive while under the influence.

It's unheard of that these double-standard word-arrangers, privileged people of this status, would sue a country club or a person who let them drive drunk after leaving their home after a private party, even if an injury or death occurred. Frankly speaking, birds of the same feather don't sue each other.

Not much is said either about a drunk who buys a twelve-pack at a carry-out and gets back on the road, but it's open season on bar and nightclub owners all year round for lawsuits and violations.

The subliminal sensationalism used in marketing violence for the last twenty-five years has made today's young people more than willing to get in a fight, just because it's cool. And there's nowhere better to experience this preprogrammed "fight club" mentality than in a bar.

When someone fights in a bar or a big fight breaks out in a larger club, and someone gets injured, the owner is liable. If someone goes outside and gets beat up, the owner is liable. When someone in security gets punched while breaking up a fight, because he's human and gets mad and kicks somebody's butt and throws them out, even though they started it and deserved it, the double-standard legal profession makes the owner liable.

The person who gets beat up will get a lawyer and sue, even when he or she was at fault and started it. Whether through in-court or out-of-court settlement by insurance company, the legal profession makes out (if they don't get a third of the settlement, they still get their fee). Just like the ambulance chasers of old, they don't care about right or wrong; their only objective is to hit someone with a lawsuit, with the bottom line being a third of the settlement.

The TV and movie industry has preprogrammed violence in young people, not caring about morals or the damage it does to young people's happiness and their parents' suffering. Because the industry is controlled by the Puppeteers, when the media present violence as a major issue it gets no further than false promises by politicians who exploited the issue for votes. Then either the politicians or the media suddenly develop amnesia and never bring up the issue again.

Another double-standard interpretation of the law used by the word-arrangers: Gambling in a bar is illegal, but gambling in a carry-out is legal.

Union

The people who can relate to my view on unions are the people who were lucky enough to be in a good union. Numerous lower-middle-class offspring became upper class because of a parent or grandparent who belonged to a union, which enabled him or her to make a fair wage and gave the security to send the kids to college.

Unions = unity. Unity is what is needed now more than ever. Americans have turned into a bunch of individualists and togetherness has just about become extinct. Everyone wants to be Number One, and will screw the other person to achieve their goal. Kids who were taught not to speak to strangers became today's grownups who are afraid to talk to strangers and usually won't even make eye contact. Looking the other way when a stranger needs help is the preprogrammed paranoid thinking of today's society.

From my invisible position behind the bar, I would listen to people from higher tax brackets who would slam unions with a jealous, hateful mindset. Most of those who consider themselves as upper class didn't realize that their livelihood depended on the lower-middle-class union workers. Other times I would listen to the pro-union blue-collar workers bitch about the rich, but with far less hate toward the upper class than that of the latter toward themselves. Each side fails to realize its necessary connection to the other. The only difference between the two was in ordering a bottle of beer or a glass of Scotch. They all wanted a better lifestyle with more security and opportunity for their children.

After years of observation and study of this behavior, it became apparent to me that the resentment brewed up between lower-middle-class and not-so-upper-class Americans is uncalled for. The low-mid and the not-so-upper-class people are in the same boat: We're the people who pay the taxes that support America and a big part of the world. The Puppeteers and all their puppets who pocket or waste our tax dollars have instilled, in low- to upper-class, the preprogrammed mindset to resent each other and fight instead of cooperate and unite.

Living in Florida, I played volleyball on the weekends and hung out on the beach with the local young adults. Afterward, we would sit around and have a few beers while shooting the shit. Every now and again, unions would pop up in conversation. Inevitably, when some young college person would start blasting unions, I would ask two questions: Where were their parents or grandparents from? Nine out of ten times, they would have an up-north union background. I would explain to them how the security of union jobs led to their enjoying the beach lifestyle. Their reply would be, that's not what they were taught at college. The second question was: Did you ever work at a place with a good union? "No" would be their answer, and mine would be, "What gives you the reason to blast unions, when having no hands-on experience on the subject?" Again the reply would be, "Well, that's what we were taught at school."

Over forty years ago, when I started working in a union shop, a person with a high school education or less couldn't have asked for better security than a union provided for raising a family. Not only a fair wage, you also got a break on prescriptions and medical expenses, as well as the protection from being fired unjustly. But from then to now, with the help of the media, movies, and our educational system, plus the government propaganda, the system has presented unions as a corrupt mafia-ridden organization, robbing workers of their unions' funds. I agree that unions have been taken over by corrupt, greedy leaders that have ruined them. It coincides with the corrupt, greedy Berkeley mafia type that has ruined our government in America.

Once union workers gained freedom, along with the freedom of thought that a steady income provided, the solidarity of union workers became an uncontrollable voting force in America. This scared the hell out of the Puppeteers. That's when they started to use all their financial strength to break unions. Whenever the financial system puts on a campaign to blow something out of the water, it's because it's afraid of it. Frankly speaking, corporations don't want cooperation, only control and submission.

Movies and TV specials about unions have put the emphasis on a corrupt Hoffa-like image. Our educational system has been teaching young students nothing but the corruption in unions, not the benefits they offer employee members. Our government, along with the media, made prosecuting a union leader a live theatrical extravaganza, with the result being tax dollars wasted on investigating committees, and number-one ratings for the media.

The uneducated, muscle-head, know-it-all union leaders in factories who can be corrupted easily are what companies and national union leaders want for scapegoats. Most factory employees with strong unions are followers who are misled by union leaders, who they want to trust. Their information comes from factory gossip and rumors, and from the 11:00 p.m. news. The only real issue to them is if they get a raise or not.

For twenty-five years I belonged to the biggest labor union in Toledo. During that time, I personally knew three or four of the men who ran our local both inside and outside the factory. Not one of them had the education or knowledge to handle the company lawyers. Behind closed doors, they sat and listened eighty percent of the time. Then they would go to union meetings and deliver phony rah-rah speeches that the followers would fall for.

In the early seventies, the union representative started getting little perks from the company. From that time on, our union went downhill fast. Because of financial gain, they worried more about pissing the company off than taking care of the union members. How could the union reps go home and tell their wives, "We're not going on the paid trips (vacations) that were called conventions, conferences, company seminars, and so on"? It was a joke to me seeing pictures of our union reps in their shiny union jackets seated at conference tables with the company people in their five-hundred-dollar suits.

A union member who was sincere and spoke the truth and got people to think (not just listen) would get elected as a union rep, but would usually be pushed aside, or would get tired of beating his head against a wall because of no help from above. If the reps got too popular and became a threat, there was a good chance they would get a visit from the "international boys," warning them about making waves. You don't have to be in a union to know the history of unions. There have been people who were threatened, beaten half to death, even killed over power struggles, or for speaking the truth. "Yes" men live longer than those who speak up and say, "That's not beneficial for the union membership."

Frankly speaking, the international union is another one of those organizations with double standards that uses union members' money to misrepresent them. I was a strong union-minded person in the late sixties and thought about pursuing a career in the union movement. I'm glad I didn't, though; you get to a point where you get discouraged. I know all about the international union goon squad. They did what they were told and their orders were passed down from the company's big boys. (The company would do what they could behind the scenes to help the muscle-heads sway union elections.)

The bad rap on unions is how they protected the dead-beats and the people who take advantage of the company because of union protection. True, but these cases are far and few between, but surely get all the publicity. The idea was sold to America that unions drove up costs. I want to know the results of the anti-union propaganda, which caused one of our big consumer products to go down in price? All that happened was that the conglomerates, with their paid-for politicians, changed tariffs and tax laws to accommodate the big companies so they could get cheap Third World labor to make the product and ship it back to America to end up with more profit. "I, for one, sure am glad they broke unions. I like buying foreign-made products of cheap quality at a higher price!"

When I moved to Florida in the mid eighties, there was still a lot of employment in union shops. Toledo wasn't as crime-ridden as it is now. It would be interesting to know how Toledo's crime rate rose more dramatically after closed factories had been replaced by Third World labor.

Now the few good, strong unions left are seeing their companies taken over by foreign industrialists through mergers. Our labor laws don't apply to these foreign companies, and they do with labor whatever they want. With the help of lawyers and union agents, Americans' rights are going out the window. People who still have a halfway decent union should be careful for whom they vote, as their future is at stake. The media do not focus on young soldiers coming home in body bags, protecting American industrial interests in Third World cheap-labor countries.

Breaking unions opened the floodgates for legislators who serve insurance companies by changing labor and safety laws to protect companies from lawsuits even when they're at fault. In the last decade or so, while the media and other Puppeteers who controlled sources of information diverted the attention of the American public, and had them glued to the tube, watching the latest scandal, tragedy, murder trial, or war, the insurance companies' word-arrangers rewrote labor and safety laws, taking away the rights of American workers. Now, laws that protected workers, whether in a union or not, are no longer in the books.

The number of industrial accidents is escalating all the time. Companies with no fear of retribution are bending or breaking safety regulations more than ever. A person who spills a cup of coffee on himself can sue for millions, but a person doing his job who gets seriously injured by a company's negligence ends up with peanuts. (I know; I just went through such an ordeal.)

OSHA has turned out to be a joke. It started out like other organizations with good intentions, but like everything else that was supposed to be good for workers, it became controlled by big money. Most industrial accidents are not even heard about unless death occurs. All OSHA does is make a lot of noise. OSHA usually turns its back on workers who are injured and gives the company a slap on the hand with some puny fine. Companies get away with injustices that strong unions wouldn't allow.

People on salary get forced to take early retirement, or are just let go.

People with twenty years of service or more are forced to take tests that the company knows those who are not computer-literate can't pass, just as an excuse to demote them, and bring in younger people at lower wages.

People are forced to work overtime, without time-and-a-half pay, or, in some cases, don't get paid for it at all. Some are being laid off when others with less seniority are allowed to work.

Ask anyone who lost his job, either by getting fired or by just being "let go" after doing a good job, if they wouldn't have liked to have had union representation.

Labor has paid the price for companies to rake in larger profits. At the same time, the American public has had to tolerate inferior products made with cheap plastic, cheap steel, cheap engineering, everything cheap but the price.

Americans have become the recipients of "Made in China" or some other twenty-five-cents-a-day, Third World country's crap: products designed to fall apart or break down a week after the warranty expires, and products that are advertised to last a lifetime, yet a warranty is recommended.

Consumers are misled with fork-tongued marketing schemes. New and Improved, Money-Back Guarantee, One-Day Sale, Going Out of Business Sale, Buy One – Get One Free. "FREE," "SALE" ... these marketing ploys can get you trampled if you're in the way of a herd of housewives (I can't believe people over forty still fall for it).

Any way you look at it, the populace should have the opportunity to vote for NAFTA, GATT, etc. rather than letting these things be decided by politicians who are controlled by special-interest lobbyists and soft money. This blow to low-mid Americans' livelihood and America's economy that world trade agreements have produced has affected all taxpayers: Increased taxes are needed to cover unemployment insurance, and unemployment results in higher crime rates, which induce higher taxes.

I reiterate, after all the bad publicity about unions being responsible for price increases, I'd like to know when the price of anything has come down since unions were legislated out of power. I know two things that went down: quality and minimum wage. Yes, there have been increases in minimum wage; however, the current minimum wage has not caught up with inflation.

Frankly, I thought the union wasn't necessary for my survival, but I realized it provided security for my children's well-being. When my kids became self-reliant young adults, I walked out of the factory to pursue other interests. For others, the union was their salvation; they wanted nothing else. It suited them wonderfully: security for the family and that reliable forty-hour paycheck every week. They were happy, took pride in their work and in being the family breadwinner. Unions hurt the filthy rich conglomerates, not America. Nobody can tell me that unions weren't good for millions of Americans. I'll be pro-union until the day I die, even though my union turned its back on me.

Legal Profession

"There's no excuse for ignorance of law." I would like to meet the person who keeps track of or has the knowledge of changes in laws at the pace the legal profession rewrites or invents them these days.

Throughout the years of tending bar, I talked and listened to people from about every line of work there is. There were always some from each profession who were unhappy with their line of work. It might be a little bit higher, but for the benefit of doubt, fifty percent of the legal professionals I dealt with didn't like what they were doing and wished they had chosen a different line of work. I have lent an ear to my share of attorneys sobbing in their drinks about how they didn't like themselves, or they knew or thought people hated them because of their profession. Possibly, it might have a lot to do with the high rate of alcoholism, drug addiction, and suicides in the legal profession.

In a book I read thirty years ago, I came across a term used to describe legal professionals. "Word-arrangers" hit the nail right on the old head. I've tried to point out how the word-arrangers control or influence most of the subjects I have given my views on throughout this book. Frankly, I think they've turned most Americans into untrusting, suspicious, paranoid, tunnel-visioned, unhappy, preprogrammed lambs being led to the slaughter.

In law schools, the word-arrangers are taught a special language partly derived from Latin and pieces of common

English. They learn to use this, altering our vocabulary to keep us in the dark. (If you can't ask me any questions, I can't tell you any lies.)

What common sense dictates doesn't count in the court unless presented in the legal professional jargon. Not knowing the word-arrangers' special lingo makes it next to impossible to defend yourself and win. There's no doubt the legal profession coined this phrase" "If you act as your own attorney, you have a fool for a client."

The legal profession caters to the wealthy, aristocratic elite, and prospers off low-mid Americans directly or through tax money. The wealthy are people who don't have a clue about the social ills, or know what it's like to hack it in the real world through hard work; they think living off the lower classes is the way it's supposed to be. These behind-the-scenes rule-makers and decision-makers are the orchestrators for the Puppeteers who use the word-arrangers to keep us confused, deceived, demoralized, and most importantly dominated.

The legal profession is not interested in the rights of people; it just wants what's right for their profession, like passing new laws and regulations that create more income for and dependency on their profession. Instead of using knowledge to straighten out social ills, we pass laws. It seems like we're passing a law to change a law that already was a law. The whole legal procedure from the attorney to judge is a planned process to prolong the inevitable on an issue that, half the time, simple logic could have resolved in a heartbeat.

The word-arrangers will drag out a case when it benefits them, but slow it to endorse a law that benefits other people. They're lightning-quick to change a law they can use against us. The legal profession's rules go way beyond double standards. I don't think they have any standards, only outrageous fees.

Two of the Puppeteers' main moneymakers and control factors are the legal profession and insurance companies. They're a two-part whole, structured by the fine print of the word-arrangers' secret language. America's insurance dependence wouldn't be so essential if it weren't for the legal profession making everybody "sue-crazy." The legal profession, by whipping up new laws and regulations to benefit insurance companies, has Americans feeling fearful and vulnerable if they don't have full coverage. (You bet your life, it's a lot of bull.)

I have a few friends who are attorneys, and I hope they stay friends. To hate a lawyer is not the point, even though it's hard not to. But we have to put the brakes on the legal profession. Its control over our lives and freedom has to change. Like any other significant change for the better, it will take time. One thing that will help is for people to quit mistaking educational status for knowledge. Most Americans accept the changes in our laws and regulations because smooth-talking, fork-tongued politicians (who are usually lawyers), along with the help of the media, sell it to the people by convincing them it's for their benefit. What people find out, when it's too late, the word-arrangers already have structured and taken care of it with their secret language of fine print, resulting in low-mid-class responsible working people paying, rather than the sleaze-ball criminal who pays nothing.

The ABA (American Bar Association) should stand for the America Boughten Association. Ethics of the legal profession are determined by their financial reward, not by right or wrong. I know there're lawyers who don't have this mindset, but they're not found on the twenty-first floor in a plush office of a high rise. It's hard for me to believe a lawyer can look in a mirror and feel proud of himself after using loopholes in the law to set a murderer free, or keep convicts on death row for so long that they have forgotten what they had done to get them there, or use their word-arranger devious skills to railroad an innocent person. And for the defense attorneys who used the minor mistakes in an investigation to set free a murderer they knew was guilty—these shysters can't commit suicide fast enough! The word-arrangers can mislead you for years, by tricking you with depositions, confusing you with legal jargon, and then telling you, "We don't have much of a case." They justify their deception with, "I'm sorry, that's the law." Because the legal profession makes the rules with their conjured-up use of words, to win or lose a case, the legal profession still wins financially.

The political word-arrangers who control whom we get to vote for have Americans accepting the fact that they're voting for a person who used illegal, unfair means to gain this position. I quit voting for presidential candidates when I realized I had to choose one of two corrupt liars who had no intention or means of helping me or low-mid America. The number-one remark that is still used as a response to my view is the subliminally preprogrammed, "Sure, they're crooks, but you have to vote for someone." More than fifty percent of the presidents were from the legal profession. I think this fact has a lot to do with why the United States has lost its unity and turned Americans into preprogrammed pawns for the Puppeteers' use.

The word-arrangers have taken the clarity and simplicity out of our decision making and turned black-and-white answers into double-standard talk and deceptive confusion, with marginal calls referred to with phrases such as "alleged," "a person of interest," "what is 'is,'" "acceptable losses," "expansionism," "soft money," "gray areas," "collateral damage," etc. Right or wrong is defined by the word-arrangers of who's in financial control—who's in charge.

The legal profession's entrenchment in the media has people watching high-profile sensational stories like the O.J. fiasco and the pecker tracks on the blue dress in the "Oral Office," while behind the scenes the legal profession and legislators change laws and pass bills that hurt Americans, like taking away patients' rights, putting loopholes in tax laws that favor conglomerates, giving more control to the police, taking away rights from citizens in their homes, allocating money for corrupt spending, and hundreds more that should be reported. By the time the truth is known, the legal profession has managed to put the burden on low-mid-class American taxpayers. "Sorry, too late, that's the law."

Legal oxymorons and obvious legal shenanigans:

• Life plus ninety-nine years
• Stalking—a serious law, or a funny movie called *10*

• Judge—someone you're supposed to respect, or a sawed-off mouthy woman who insults you with derogatory written remarks.

• High-profile cases—high-priced word-arrangers who swarm like sharks in a feeding frenzy. An everyday innocent person gets a public defender.

• The results of most lawsuits are known by the word-arrangers long before the client.

• Presidents have become a pardoning board.

• A bad childhood is an excuse for premeditated murder of children, to escape the proper punishment.

• Military spokesman—a word-arranger who knows more about the military than an officer with years of experience.

• Killed by "friendly" fire—That sure makes a parent feel better.

• The word-arranger called "hospital spokesman" must know more than the veteran physicians.

• Soft money—payments for a favor needed later.

By misconstruing the use of the word "freedom" in our Constitution, the legal profession shows how greed overpowers their decision-making on morals and the real meaning of freedom.

The controversy that entangles the deep-rooted social, political, and financial problems revolves around the legal profession. The purpose behind the word-arrangers' rhetoric and double standards is to keep low-mid Americans in a maze of deception, disagreement, and discontent. I could fill a book on the legal profession being responsible for stress, depression, financial pressure, and loss of unity in low-mid America. This loss of unity has enabled the legal profession to use special-interest groups over the majority's best interests on issues that benefit the wealthy and the legal profession, rather than America.

At one time, a sense of fair play with simple logic to help obtain a just solution for judgment on right or wrong weighed heavy on the scales of justice. Today, they carry little or no weight at all in our double-standard court system.

I have to make last call on this subject. Frankly speaking, I hope calling the legal profession into my life will not be necessary, but that's unlikely. In my judgment, the legal profession is on the bottommost rung of the ladder of human compassion.

Positions for Profit

The medicine men of early cultures used their alleged knowledge of the unknown and other's ignorance of the unknown to help keep their tribes' people in control for the benefit of the chiefs. We might think we're far advanced from such early cultures, but we're still ignorant about who is in control and how they control us. The M in AMA (American Medical Association) should stand for "marionette." The board members of the AMA are representatives of drug companies, financial institutions, and a few physicians who sit on boards of the hospital industry controlled by the Puppeteers. Their decision on what's healthy for Americans has nothing to do with health, but only with wealth. Having the legal profession and the medical profession in their back pockets, the Puppeteers have two of the most powerful and lucrative organizations for controlling their overabundant wealth.

The AMA board's financially motivated members' manipulations and high cost of medical care are just as dishonorable as any terrorist act.

The burden put by the AMA on the elderly for the cost of the prescription drugs they need to maintain good health is criminal. These are people who have supported America all their lives. Their devotion is rewarded by the government turning its back on them, letting them get shafted by drug lords and the financiers of the AMA.

By far, one of the most overpriced businesses in America is health care, particularly hospitals. They get away with discrimination, and no politician possesses the honesty or power needed to point a guilty finger in their direction, the main reasons being that no politicians will bite the hand that feeds them. The Puppeteers that profit from hospitals' dishonest price-gouging techniques are the same people who control most of our politicians.

Hospitals greet you with open arms if you're rich or have full-coverage insurance. You're rushed in, have twenty-five x-rays, doctors hover over you with all the special attention. Then they put you in a nice expensive room where you get two aspirins that cost ten dollars apiece. If you don't have the right coverage or have little more than the shirt on your back, no matter how serious your ailment or injury, you have a good chance of getting turned away by a lot of hospitals. Frankly, it's un-American that so many Americans are going untreated because of financial fear, not fear of their medical problems.

The people who had no light at the end of the tunnel, whom Dr. Kevorkian assisted in suicide, had the right to make their own personal choice between suffering or a quick, painless death. It wasn't offending religion or breaking the long-forgotten meaning of the Hippocratic oath that landed this Good Samaritan in jail. It was the behind-the-scenes power of the AMA and its public opinion maker, the media, that pushed for his prosecution.

The AMA wants people to die in a hospital or nursing home where they can drag it out for financial gain, not caring a hoot about the indignity and suffering of the patient or the pain the loved ones have to endure.

I've read surveys that say we're living longer than past generations. Even though most of the surveys in one way or another are paid for by the AMA, it's true. But I question the later years of our lives. I know more people my age and younger who will need a pharmacy the rest of their lives than people who won't. We've been living longer by pushing drugs, not pushing health.

These extra years that people are living now are no different from the last years of people's lives fifty years ago. For most, the results are the same. They end up hospital- and drug-dependent, degraded and broke. If the number-one priority were teaching preventative measures for the good health of our bodies and minds, along with proper nutrition in our younger years, a person's last years would be healthier and happier. Teaching children how to avoid and deal with the number-one killer, stress and depression, and how it breaks the body down making it vulnerable to hereditary disease, is just as important as teaching them their ABCs. Frankly speaking, real wealth is enjoying good health in later years.

The teaching of bureaucratic survival in medical schools is as much a part of future physicians' curriculum as medicine. Physicians, like lawyers, are taught a secret language. A big part of their schooling is learning part Latin and part words from our language to disguise the idea we're familiar with. This technique enabled the AMA to add another money-maker to the medical profession, the pharmacist. The druggist is the last leg of the AMA's drug distribution network.

Only one other profession has as much responsibility for influence over life and death in America as the medical profession. Physicians' good intentions and dedication to health and accountability for right and wrong are, at best, secondary to pushing the latest drug the AMA dictates them to. The AMA's control over every area of their professional lives handicaps them from being healers first. The AMA standards they have to abide by give them no choice but to think of patients as livelihood first, and only next as people in need of care, concern, and attention.

• Not long ago, your family doctor was like a good mechanic. He knew how to fix it. Now doctors, like mechanics, insist on a diagnostic readout for specialized repair. It used to be your doctor or on to the hospital; very seldom were you sent to a specialist. Now your doctor serves as a middleman for the specialist and the pharmacist. Your doctor agrees with you after being told what the problem is and then you are off to the specialist! Ring up the cost of one office call. Frankly speaking, let's hope the bar business never adopts this type of rip-off service. You could get charged to order a drink, then charged again to have it mixed.

It takes a different kind of dedication to treat pus-filled sores, and look at nasty rectums and babies dying. I commend the physicians who endure this because they want to care for people. They take the Hippocratic oath to heart. But in the medical profession and the legal profession there are too many people who pick these professions primarily for financial rewards. If these two professions don't clean up their acts in the future, physicians won't be able to afford malpractice insurance for their assembly-line methods of making more money. Lawyers won't be able to afford or have enough security to keep all the clients they have screwed from getting revenge.

• Nurses, all grief and no glory. I've heard people complain that nurses get paid too much. Frankly, they couldn't pay me enough to do what they do. They're the real unsung heroes in the medical profession. I think they're extraordinary, up near the top on the ladder of human compassion.

Even this once dedicated profession has yielded to hospitals' "time and space are money" assembly-line practices. This megabucks medical monopoly that's become a new major source of employment has made the rewards of self-gratification in the nursing profession lose ground to the monetary rewards. It reminds me of the grumpy assembly-line worker I saw in the factory who didn't like his job, but it paid well.

• A psychiatrist—you want to talk about a depressing job? (It would be like having to watch the Lifetime TV channel all day, every day.) Having to listen to people's problems day after day could make a person want to drink, a lot. At least a bartender can say, "Excuse me, I have a customer waiting," and go to the other end of the bar to escape. I can remember only a couple of psychiatrists as customers. I might have had more, but they just didn't want to let anyone know their profession.

Psychiatrists have you pay for ten visits before telling you what your problem is, when they know after one or two. It's somewhat questionable. The real mind-blower is the power they have over people's lives with their testimony in courts. By saying someone has "a history of mental problems," they can keep a person who's a premeditated murderer, "guilty as sin," from getting the punishment he deserves. After only a few hours of conversation and reading a one-sided view of an individual, they have all the answers, and use their secret-language malarkey that the courts call "expert testimony" to get an insanity plea to keep another murderer alive. It's strange they can't do the same thing for patients without the need for ten visits or more.

Every profession that prospers by getting its hands on government tax money also becomes a costly nightmare for low-mid Americans. Being part of the AMA network of "potions for profit" distributors, psychiatrists administer drugs to schoolchildren with the school system's encouragement and government backing. This is a prescription for the bureaucratic budget and the AMA to get well "healed." Time and teaching methods for rehabilitation are replaced with a drug.

Knowing all the bad side-effects from stimulants and amphetamines that children will face, psychiatrists and school officials pressure parents (who don't have the knowledge or don't take the time necessary to handle a problem child) into these drug programs, sometimes without parents' approval, being overruled by a money-motivated force in regard to their children's well-being.

Raises for administrators, and overpriced drugs and psychiatrist's fees are things the educational budget has no trouble coming up with, but money for teachers and school programs to help children in their difficult years get set aside. "Sorry, the school levy didn't pass."

Frankly speaking, this bartender listened to people's problems and administers a drug as psychiatrists do. Besides lacking a college degree, the difference is: This bartender didn't tell people a drug would help solve their problems.

• Like the AMA, the FDA (Food and Drug Administration) is another organization run by puppets of corporate America, who are controlled by the purse strings of the Puppeteers. These executives from the sugar industry, major food companies, drug companies, and financiers have the last word on what's healthy for Americans; their set of rules and regulations and their greed-infected minds have been poisoning Americans ever since the FDA came into existence. Drug companies are one of the main benefactors of the FDA and AMA's double-standard guidelines. The drug companies' financial control of the FDA and AMA is the reason there's a bigger mark-up in pharmaceutical drugs than in diamonds.

The government's failure to govern and control the drug companies is just another form of corruption of our elected officials, who really work for their under-the-table and soft-money contributors from the drug industry, to whom they owe favors. During the 2000 election, the drug industry contributed more than eighteen million dollars to politicians from *both* parties. That's called "covering your ass." Also, taxpayers' money is used by government agencies to enforce the FDA's version of health, to protect the financial empires of the FDA drug lords.

The FDA disregards warnings from outside medical experts on drugs that are harmful and sometimes life-threatening, while talking about the latest miracle drug they rush to get on the market, without proper testing, unless you call tests based on whether a rat lives or dies good enough. If one takes a drug to relieve one ailment, one has to suffer hair loss, nausea, stomach bleeding, heart failure, liver damage, "erectionlessness," and so on. Big pharmaceutical companies spent $1.7 billion on TV ads in 2000, filling the airwaves with lies, selling themselves as compassionate humanitarians. Good guys they're not. They're in the same category as the huckster medicine men of old, who sold their cure-all snake oil with false promises. Maybe we should bring back the tar and feathers, and ride them out of town on a rail.

• The AMA always was and still is against chiropractic and applied kinesiology assistance for some health problems; the reason for this is that they don't want people to know that some ailments can be cured without drugs. For years, I've been going to an applied kinesiologist for treatment of back and neck injuries. I know for sure I would have been under the knife a long time ago, like friends and people I work with, if I were treated by a regular M.D., resulting in nerve damage from operations and a lifetime of drugs. They're not a cure-all for everybody's health problems, but they deserve more credit than they get. Personally, I wouldn't be in the good shape I'm

in today without applied kinesiology. Thank you Dr. Grady
(D.C., applied kinesiologist).

• After my mother passed away from diabetes, in 1976, I
read book after book and every magazine about this awful
disease. In 1979, while I was being treated for a back injury, my
kinesiologist gave me a book to read called *Sugar Blues*. I can't
put into words the effect this book had on me. It was my first
eye-opener on how powerful the sugar industry is. Twenty-
some years later, I can state with strong conviction that the
best-kept secret is that sugar kills more people than any drug
out there. It would take another book for me to explain the
evils of sugar and the sugar industry. But I will give you a
thousand to one odds that the FDA will never tell you.

Last Call

I love America. It's the greatest country in the world, and
that's why most want to live here. It's more than monetary and
material advantages that draw people here from all over the
world. The thing that made America the greatest country in
the world is *freedom*, freedom of choice, freedom of speech,
and, most of all, the opportunities that freedom provides.
Being "a man of means, by no means," and from an insignificant background, I felt grateful for the freedom to openly
express my views, based on my bartending experience and free-
spirited lifestyle.

I believe low-mid Americans can eliminate the preprogrammed mindset of pointing unforgiving fingers at each other
over disagreements that arise from variety in the cultural influ-
ences in our diversity by opening that versatile toolbox, the
brain, which has all the tools to repair the biggest share of
personal and social disharmonies in low-mid America. Taking
a little time to pursue the knowledge that the information
highway provides in this multiple-outlet age, Americans can re-
establish some much-needed unity and quit having to pay for,
and have, their lives be regulated by the whims of special-
interest groups. It's most unfortunate that a sensationalized
issue makes the media and lobbyists more important than the
will of the majority. I'm not trying to push my views down

anyone's throat. The preprogramming of low-mid Americans to jump through hoops took years to make and most assuredly it will take years to break. Nevertheless, the solutions are right before our eyes, if you open that toolbox and start using all your own tools. (Government of the people, by the people, for the people—let's not forget this, low-mid Americans.)

From the time humans began to walk upright to keep from getting their hands dirty, we've been on a quest to make the labor of living easier. Now our complex product-obsolescence system has replaced trial and error with "time is money," quantity instead of quality. This modern-day standard doesn't always result in making *our lives* easier, but it does result in making a profit easier. Profit is the most important part of our economic structure; in one way or another, it's what most strive for. But when does the bottom line stop and greed take over? When are too many zeroes after the comma too many?

The old saying "Necessity is the mother of invention" has become passé; the meaning doesn't have the same prestige or intention it used to. Now it's "Stick it to the consumer," perpetrated by greedy manufacturers' engineering methodology, resulting in habitual product obsolescence.

The unnecessary gadgets believed to be necessary and marketed (hustled) to today's paranoid got-to-have-it mindset have turned into "a mother of nuisance." The myth about making your life easier has heightened our dependency on gadgets. This dependency has weakened the last few generations of Americans.

The effect of this easy, lazy lifestyle has impaired some human strengths and character-builders that reinsure our confidence and individuality. It befuddles me observing young adults being lost without their calculators, not being able to do simple math in their heads. Relying on easier, quicker gadgets that eliminate the physical benefits of labor has produced inactive, unhealthy, lacking-in-self-fortitude young adults. In some, not having the latest or mainstream marketed craze, others' approval, and peer pressure result in a self-induced feeling of inferiority or insecurity.

Frankly speaking, by the time a gadget is marketed-to-the-max to consumers, it's already been made obsolete by the new technology that's ready and waiting to be unleashed. All people, including me, fall prey to marketing gimmicks, to indulge in something we don't need. It's a happiness that's all-American.

The marketers know low-mid Americans have money to squander. They must sit behind closed doors busting a gut over the way "gotta have it mania" has them preprogrammed. Low-mid Americans complain about the economy, rising taxes, higher utility and fuel prices, the whole rip-off domino effect that seems to have no end. At the same time, low-mid Americans spend money on no-brainer telephone polls and rigged surveys, names engraved on a grain of rice, towels to wave, lotto tickets, speaker systems and rims that can cost as much as the car in some cases, brand names and logos more essential than the value of the items, and other absurd materialistic expenditures. Americans' thoughtless abuse of natural resources and excessive use of energy and commodities has made America the world's largest producers of waste and wasters. A good example that comes to mind: driving with lights on in the daylight. If your vision is that bad, take a cab.

Americans have to rearrange their thinking and apply more common sense to break the control over their time and thinking to deprogram themselves from their false-value spending addiction for the latest craze's gadget. The potential of technology along with the brain is handicapped by time and money; ultimately neither will be held back.

In today's society, it's all about numbers, but the number that causes people more frustration and stress and the one people are in blind pursuit of is the number "one." People have to be the right one, the only one, the first one, got to have one, the best one, and the paranoid biggie, "I'm not Number One." People diligently strive to be politically correct, be in the mainstream, part of the "in" crowd, keep up with the Joneses, missing the simple pleasures right at their fingertips, struggling to impress and please everyone but the right one—themselves.

I've relived a good share of my life writing *Frankly Speaking*. After all is said and done, other than more hair in my ears and nose, I haven't changed a great deal. What worked for me was a good, positive attitude, being a people-person, enjoying laughter and good times, and possessing a good sense of humor. I feel fortunate enough to have grown up in the three-channel TV happy days, when people said "Thank you" instead of "Forget you." A man could open a door for a woman or smile at a toddler without people thinking he had ulterior motives.

I can't explain the natural ability I have for dealing with people, or why I am open-minded, put unpleasantness in a light perspective, have an uncanny facility for listening to and observing people who, quite often, were out of sync or at their worst. I do know these attributes were the springboard for my propensity to study people.

I conducted my own case studies on friends and customers, watching them get stressed out over what was out of their control and seeing how it crippled their bodies and minds. It helped establish my own standards for happiness, which proved invaluable for good health as the years passed by. I usually start out liking everyone, but if a person proves different, I don't get close enough for dislike.

I taught myself a mental catchphrase I used when a person was rude, obnoxious, inconsiderate, or showed any other kind of weakness: I never want to be like them.

When asked, "Are you all right?" if I was discouraged or disappointed, my reply would be, "No, but I *will* be."

• If there ever was a lesson that a bartender learned real quick, it was "You can't please everyone." I was privileged to have a knack for letting the bad things in my past stay in the past.

• Our government is a prime example of the old saying, "Promises are made to be broken."

• I feel privileged to have friends to drink with in low-mid places.

• I never give much thought about mountains to climb, just different roads to travel.

• Love should be a feeling, not a proclamation used for procurement.

• I don't see anything wrong with looking at the world through rose-colored glasses.

• There are more good customers in the world than bad.

My not thinking that it is essential to possess material things has puzzled my family and friends. I never had a desire to pursue wealth; I chose health. It's not that I have anything against money; money is to spend and that's what I like to do with it. I liked the way Walter Hagan (a golfer in the thirties and forties) said it: "I don't want to be a millionaire, just live like one." I'm happier spending money on my loved ones and whatever my feelings tell me to do with it than I would be trying to put more zeroes behind the comma in a checkbook.

Throughout the years, my spending habits have been thought of as a weakness by many of my acquaintances. Most of the people I have known who thought money was their security blanket and guaranteed the "good life" later found out that it didn't have the value they thought it had, compared to having good health and happiness. Frankly speaking, I value the thought that I am my future.

If I had the power to mix up a magical cocktail for the people of the world to drink, one I believe would make for a better world, it would consist of four ingredients.

Here's the recipe:

1 part—Make greed extinct
1 part—We're all the same color
1 part—Religion is secondary
1 part—The masses are as dumb as I

Down the hatch! It's closing time.

EPILOGUE

by Dr. Ramakrishna Puligandla

Now that you have read the book, you are in a position to make your own judgment about and evaluation of it. Frank and I most earnestly hope that you have enjoyed the book, regardless of any differences you may have with Frank on a variety of topics. He is fully aware that he has discussed many sensitive issues and expressed his own views and judgments, which the reader may not agree with. What Frank has to say in this book is entirely based on his firsthand experience as a bartender, not on hearsay, rumor, bias, and prejudice.

Many people think that a bartender should simply tend bars and not pretend to be a social critic. Such a view of a bartender, to say the least, is based on stereotyping bartenders as people who lack the intelligence and ability to be social critics; I hereby submit that people who think of bartenders in this manner are wholly mistaken, for bartenders, simply by virtue of their occupation, have the extraordinary opportunities to directly interact with people from various strata of society and become confidants, shrinks, and confessors, thereby gaining remarkable insights into human nature and society in general. Frank is not just a bartender; he is also a highly skilled journeyman millwright; above all, he is a very intelligent person and acquires a lot of knowledge through reading and discussions on the most complex matters of human life, society, government, history, and so on.

Let me emphasize that this does not mean that everyone has to agree with Frank on what he has to say; rather, it only means that Frank has honestly and boldly put forward his own views and judgments, thereby provoking others to examine and evaluate their own views and judgments on a large number of important matters concerning the individual human being and society in general.

Printed in the United States
34753LVS00003B/58-66

9 781587 364792